DEVELOPING VISUAL LITERACY
in Science, K–8

DEVELOPING VISUAL LITERACY

in Science, K–8

Jo Anne Vasquez
Michael W. Comer
Frankie Troutman

NSTApress
National Science Teachers Association
Arlington, VA

National Science Teachers Association

Claire Reinburg, Director
Jennifer Horak, Managing Editor
Andrew Cooke, Senior Editor
Judy Cusick, Senior Editor
Wendy Rubin, Associate Editor
Amy America, Book Acquisitions Coordinator

ART AND DESIGN
Will Thomas Jr., Director
Cover and interior design by Will Thomas Jr.
"Foldables" in chapters 1, 5, 6, 7, and 8 by Frankie Troutman
Cover Credits:
Praying Mantis (p. 72): *SXC.hu*, HAAP Media Ltd.
Moon Phases (p. 94): Foldable by Frankie Troutman
Plant Cell (p. 9): Hackett, J. K., R. H. Moyer, and J. Vasquez. 2008. *Science A Closer Look*. Grade 5, Visual Literacy.
    Columbus, OH: Macmillan/McGraw Hill, p. 24. Copyright © 2008 Macmillan/McGraw-Hill. Reprinted with permission.

PRINTING AND PRODUCTION
Catherine Lorrain, Director

NATIONAL SCIENCE TEACHERS ASSOCIATION
Francis Q. Eberle, PhD, Executive Director
David Beacom, Publisher

LIBRARY OF CONGRESS CATALOGING-IN-PUBLICATION DATA
Vasquez, Jo Anne, 1943-
Developing visual literacy in science, K-8 / by Jo Anne Vasquez, Michael W. Comer, and Frankie Troutman.
    p. cm.
Includes bibliographical references and index.
ISBN 978-1-935155-22-5
1. Science--Study and teaching (Elementary)--United States. 2. Science--Study and teaching (Middle school)--United States.
3. Language arts (Elementary)--United States. 4. Language arts (Middle school)--United States. 5. Visual literacy--Study and
teaching (Elementary)--United States. 6. Visual literacy--Study and teaching (Middle school)--United States I. Comer, Michael
W., 1956- II. Troutman, Frankie, 1948- III. National Science Teachers Association. IV. Title.
LB1585.3.V37 2010
372.3'5--dc22
                    2010024752

eISBN 978-1-936137-58-9

*Featuring SciLinks®—Up-to-the minute online content, classroom ideas, and other materials are just a click away. For
more information go to* www.scilinks.org/faq.aspx.

CONTENTS

FOREWORD

More than 200 years ago, Napoleon Bonaparte said, "Un bon croquis vaut mieux qu'un long discours" (A good sketch is better than a long speech). Perhaps this phrase was the origin of the popular adage "A picture is worth a thousand words." The concept certainly holds true today in preschool settings, K–12 classrooms, universities, science museums, and any place where children and adults engage in learning science.

Teachers today are working with learners who are members of the "Eye Generation"—that is, young people who are used to receiving much of their information through images (often referred to as "visual texts"). Thus it is essential that science teachers acquire the understandings, tools, and resources to support student learning and to help students become active—rather than passive—viewers of the thousands of graphic images in their worlds. Although I am aware of several published educational resources on visual literacy, *Developing Visual Literacy in Science, K–8* is the first book I have seen that specifically addresses visual literacy in the context of K–8 science. Now educators have a comprehensive resource on visual literacy that mirrors effective science instruction.

Science teachers might ask: With the growing array of skills and knowledge we already have to develop, use, and refine, why do we need to add visual literacy to the many learning approaches we must balance and use every day? The answer is that our students live in a multimedia environment that inundates them with visual imagery. A picture cannot tell a thousand words if students lack the skills to interpret and make sense—or, make meaning—of the images they encounter. The authors of this book—experienced science educators Jo Anne Vasquez, Michael Comer, and Frankie Troutman—provide practical tools and approaches that teachers can use to introduce their students to the critical skills of visual literacy. The authors also discuss the research findings that support the teaching of visual strategies.

FOREWORD

This book shows how to create graphic organizers with simple paper-folding techniques, and it presents a variety of scientific photographs, diagrams, charts, and graphs that teachers can use to go beyond text to help students access, analyze, and communicate information. These three abilities—accessing, analyzing, and communicating information—ought to be infused into all inquiry-based science lessons, with the ultimate goal of achieving science literacy in the K–8 classroom. The knowledge that teachers gain from this book will help them become better at choosing which graphic images to bring into their classrooms and deciding which images to use or not use from the textbook and other school-provided materials. Having a critical eye for representations—especially those that are inaccurate or may unintentionally convey a misconception—is extremely important to science teachers. Some visual images not only confuse students but also can reinforce the preconceptions they may bring to their learning.

Because visual literacy is an area of science education largely ignored in preservice teacher preparation and professional development, this book fills a critical void. One of the best ways to address this void in our schools is to read and share this book within a professional learning community (PLC) in your school. Coming together with other teachers (and administrators) as a PLC provides an opportunity for powerful learning around the ideas in this book. In PLCs, teachers can articulate important visual literacy skills across grade levels and collaborate on ways to successfully make visual literacy an integral component of the school's science program.

As adults, we use visual cues every day. For that reason, I hope this book is as much of a personal venture for you as it is a professional one. As one of my favorite Rod Stewart songs says, "Every picture tells a story, don't it." I hope this book will help you find ways to visually unfold the "story of science" to your students so that they may better appreciate, understand, and use science throughout their lives.

Page Keeley
Maine Mathematics and Science Alliance
NSTA President 2008–2009

ABOUT THE AUTHORS

Jo Anne Vasquez has many years of experience in K–12 science education. She holds a bachelor of science in biology, a master's in early childhood education, and a PhD in curriculum and instruction. She was a K–5 classroom teacher and a K–12 district science specialist for the Mesa (Arizona) Public Schools, where she helped develop Mesa's nationally recognized hands-on science program. She has been an adjunct professor of science education at Arizona State University and was the director of professional development and outreach for ASU's Center for Research on Education in Science, Mathematics, Engineering, and Technology (CRESMET) before joining the Helios Education Foundation in 2008. At the foundation, she is vice president and program director for Teacher and Curriculum Initiatives for Transition Years, focusing on grades 5–12 STEM (science, technology, engineering, and mathematics) education.

Jo Anne is a past president of the National Science Teachers Association and the National Science Education Leadership Association and was a Presidential Appointee to the National Science Board, the governing board of the National Science Foundation. She has won numerous awards for her contributions to the advancement of science education. In 2006, she received the National Science Teachers Association's most prestigious member award: the Robert H. Carlton Award for National Leadership in Science Education. She has also received NSTA's Distinguished Service to Science Education Award and, in 2007, the New York Academy of Science's Willard Jacobson Award for major contributions to the field of science education. In 2004, she was a NALEO (National Association of Latino Elected and Appointed Officials) honoree for her contributions to the improvement of science education.

Michael W. Comer is the national marketing manager for Macmillan/McGraw-Hill Science K–6. He previously taught elementary and middle school science in Dobbs Ferry, New York, and East Providence, Rhode Island. In his classrooms, Michael was one of the early advocates for the use of inquiry-based programs such as Science Curriculum Improvement Study and Elementary Science Study. He caught the attention of Delta Education, the providers of these curriculum materials, and joined their sales team in 1987.

Michael graduated from American International College in Springfield, Massachusetts, in 1979, with a major in biology and a minor in history. He has presented and been a guest speaker at numerous science teacher gatherings in the northeastern United States, including at M.A.S.S. (Massachusetts Association of Science Supervisors) meetings and M.A.S.T. (Massachusetts Association of Science Teachers) conventions. Farther afield, he has been a presenter at NSTA national and area conferences in Boston, St. Louis, Tulsa, and Baltimore. From 1989 to 1998 Michael helped organize and run the yearly Summer Science Seminar at Bridgewater (Massachusetts) State College. In this hands-on, graduate-level seminar, elementary teachers gained practical experience in the development of inquiry-based science lessons. Michael has also conducted science workshops in Puerto Rico, Saudi Arabia, Bahrain, and the Dutch island territory of St. Marteen.

Frankie Troutman is the curriculum director for Bright Beginnings Charter School (preK to grade 6) in Chandler, Arizona. In 2008, she retired after 38 years as a primary teacher with the Mesa (Arizona) Public Schools. During those years, she conducted numerous interactive teacher workshops on science teaching. As an expert in primary science education, she is frequently asked to present at state and national conferences.

Frankie holds a bachelor's degree in elementary education and a master's in early childhood education. She is in high demand as a professional and curriculum developer and has authored four preschool and primary science activity books published by Macmillan/McGraw-Hill. She is an active member of NSTA, the Arizona Science Teachers Association, and the National Association for the Education of Young Children.

INTRODUCTION

During a rehearsal of Claude Debussy's *La Mer*, famed Italian conductor Arturo Toscanini found himself unable to describe the effect he hoped to achieve from a particular passage. After a moment's thought, he took a silk handkerchief from his pocket and tossed it high into the air. The orchestra, mesmerized, watched the slow, graceful descent of the silken square. Toscanini smiled with satisfaction as it finally settled on the floor. "There," he said, "play it like that" (Fadiman 1985, p. 548).

A visual image gives meaning to words and offers an alternative to words as a means of communication. In schools today, the ability to read and interpret visual images and representations has become a critical learning skill, for when words and visual elements are closely tied, they help students comprehend and synthesize new information. *Visual literacy* is this ability to read and interpret visual images and, just like language and mathematical literacy, is now considered a critical part of students' must-have competencies.

Too often, educators give more weight to the verbal or linguistic way of processing knowledge than to the visual, leaving students to generate their own visual representations in order to make meaning or convey what they know and understand. Teachers may mistakenly assume that students understand what meaning a photograph, chart, or diagram is conveying. Fortunately, there is now a growing body of research, including longitudinal studies, centered on the importance of developing visual literacy and spatial-thinking skills and the implications of these skills for understanding and information retention. *Developing Visual Literacy in Science, K–8* is based on this body of research and is a professional improvement guide and resource tool for the teaching of visual literacy strategies.

This book is intended for K–8 teachers (in particular, teachers who may be new to the subject of visual literacy), prospective teachers, and teacher educators. Its purpose is to develop an awareness of the mental processes involved in interpreting visuals and to provide strategies for helping students make more effective use of visual or spatial organizational tools. Focused on the visual literacy skill development of the educator, this book examines the visual literacy research, provides examples to

INTRODUCTION

help interpret the research, and includes practice for the application of visual literacy skills.

Each of the three practice chapters (Chapters 6–8) focuses on a single aspect of life, Earth, and physical science (insect metamorphosis, phases of the Moon, and force and motion) and offers partial visual literacy lessons for use in these areas. Please keep in mind that this book does not attempt to create complete inquiry-based lessons; rather, it focuses on the content-development phase of a lesson, during which visual literacy skills can be learned and applied.

Why Students Need Visual Literacy Skills

In a recent report on skills needed in the American workforce, the National Center on Education and the Economy (2008) stated that although so-called basic literacy skills are still necessary for adult workers, *they are not sufficient* for people to become "knowledge workers" in a globally competitive marketplace. Rather,

> this is a world in which comfort with ideas and abstractions is the passport to a good job, in which creativity and innovation are the keys to the good life, in which high levels of education—a very different kind of education than most of us have had—are going to be the only security there is. (pp. 6–7)

Teachers must come to grips with this growing emphasis on what students can *do* with knowledge rather than on just what units of knowledge they have. This shift reflects the revised version of Bloom's taxonomy (Anderson and Krathwohl 2001). In Bloom's original taxonomy (or classification) of the six levels of cognitive complexity (Bloom and Krathwohl 1956), "evaluation" was at the top of the familiar pyramid—indicating that evaluation (i.e., "Can the student justify a stand or decision?") was the highest level of cognitive complexity. In the revised version, "creating" is at the top of the pyramid (i.e., "Can the student use existing information to come up with something entirely original—a new idea, a unique product, an alternative solution that is tied to a goal or a problem to be solved?"). To achieve this high level of cognition requires the abilities to process, organize, and assimilate new knowledge. Visual literacy—which calls on the viewer to interpret, demonstrate, and apply learning to new situations—is an example of the highest level of "creating" as reflected in the pyramid. Furthermore, many of our students will one day compete in a global environment in which multiple languages are spoken; to over-come language barriers, they will depend on visuals to convey information, ideas, and complex concepts.

In our experiences in K–8 classes, visual literacy is becoming recognized as a vital set of skills to have. According to early research on teaching visual literacy skills and the benefits to student understanding (Roblyer 1998), a visually literate student should be able to

- resist the manipulative use of images in advertisement and similar contexts;
- interpret, understand, and appreciate the meaning of visual messages;
- communicate more effectively by applying the basic principles and concepts of visual design;
- produce visual messages using computers and other technologies; and
- use visual thinking to conceptualize solutions to problems.

The process of becoming visually literate is not unlike the process of learning to read. It involves the learner's ability to interpret and create visual information, to understand images of all kinds, to use images to communicate more effectively, and to apply visual representations as a means for mastery and long-term retention of knowledge. Visual tools such as concept maps and graphic organizers[*] can provide one of the most direct routes for learners, especially in inclusive classrooms, to show, and communicate with, their unique patterns of thinking.

Approaches to Visual Literacy Instruction

Many people referred to the early 1990s as the "information age," an era during which knowledge was the primary industry, the industry that in fact drove the economy. The pace of societal change has accelerated even more with the advent of the digital age. We are now teaching the so-called millennium generation—that is, students who were practically born with a mouse in their hands and who have access to more information in one year than their grandparents had in a lifetime. These students are bombarded daily by visual images: short bytes of information from the TV, web-based social-networking pages, internet browsing, text messages, and tweets—and who knows what else to come!

We need to provide this generation of visual learners with abilities and techniques to help them acquire and remember the basic infor-

---

[*] See page 45 for more on concept maps; see Chapter 5 for more on graphic organizers.

mation they need so that they can become the thinkers and problem solvers of tomorrow. Of course, in no way can we as educators give them all the information they will need; the internet is the great information provider. What we must do instead is equip them with the foundational knowledge they need in order to understand what all this new information means and how to apply it to new situations. Visual literacy tools such as photographs, charts, diagrams, and graphic symbols, which can be called *visual texts* because they each represent an abstract concept or series of concepts (just like alphabetic text), are the tools that will lead this generation to become proficient in the demands of the digital age.

As of this writing, linguistic literacy (i.e., deriving meaning from written or oral language) is still the major means of learning in our schools. And although the importance of helping students develop visual literacy (i.e., deriving meaning from images or illustrations) is slowly being acknowledged by educators, research shows that students do not acquire overnight the ability to read visual images:

> The visual language has its own norms and structures, as does verbal language. Images cannot be considered trivially understandable and transparent. Misuse of the visual language can affect the communication of the concepts intended to be represented by the image. Thus, on one hand, an image that has not been well designed may transmit wrong ideas and, on the other hand, a lack of knowledge of the visual language may hinder the interpretations of an image. (Pinto and Ametller 2002, p. 335)

Fortunately, since the 1990s, one type of visual tool—the concept map—has been used widely and successfully in classrooms.

> The use of one-dimensional visual graphic organizers such as concept maps has in the past few years become widely accepted by teachers at all grade levels. Teachers have found that they are a powerful tool in the struggle to help students organize and convert information into meaningful displays for recall and retention. They have become an essential weapon in the struggle against info-glut and info-garbage. (McKenzie 1998, p. 26)

Another visual tool—the three-dimensional graphic organizer—also has proved to be an excellent way to introduce students to visual learning. Three-dimensional visual organizers leverage learning well beyond the common "linear" or one-dimension models. These organizers, commonly called *foldables*, are based on the work of our colleague, the science educator, inventor, and author Dinah Zike. Dinah has energized teaching and learning by introducing her foldables into classrooms across the country. Her work provided the basis for the other types of graphic organizers. (See page 53, "Teaching the Way You Want to Be Taught," for a first-person account by Dinah of how she came to develop foldables—first for her own use, then for her students'.)

The authors of this book have considerable experience with the application of three-dimensional organizers and we discuss them at length (see especially Chapter 5). Strategies such as three-dimensional graphic organizers can help students at all levels organize large amounts of information and support the development of their understanding of the big ideas of science.

Organization of This Book

Chapter 1: Visual Literacy: The Primer. This chapter is an overview of the concept of visual literacy and of the skill sets needed for a child or adult to be considered visually literate. The chapter provides research that supports the idea that visual literacy is one of the must-have skills of the 21st century. We use a photograph, an illustration, a Venn diagram, and a three-dimensional graphic organizer to demonstrate ways that students can be introduced to the concept of visual literacy.

Chapter 2: Interpreting Photographs. A single still photographic image can easily communicate a vast amount of information. A photograph can capture the meaning of a complex idea or concept that would require many pages of text to describe. This chapter provides you with strategies and questioning techniques to help your students learn to take full advantage of photographs in order to better understand science concepts.

Chapter 3: Interpreting Diagrams. Students encounter a variety of diagrams in their lives that convey a variety of scientific and technical information. This chapter reviews the skills and techniques necessary for analyzing and interpreting diagrams of several levels of complexity.

Chapter 4: Creating Visual Thinking Tools. When we help our students discover tools and techniques for organizing the vast amount of information we present to them, they will be much better prepared to recall, retell, or make meaning from text. In this chapter, we examine brainstorm webs, graphic organizers, and concept maps.

Chapter 5: Three-Dimensional Graphic Organizers ("Foldables"). A foldable is a three-dimensional graphic organizer that allows learners to record and process new words and concepts in a hands-on, kinesthetic way. It helps increase students' visual-spatial learning, which research has shown to be critical to long-term understanding. This chapter provides an overview of the research, gives examples of three-dimensional graphic organizers, and suggests applications of the use of this tool in science lessons.

Chapter 6: Visual Literacy in Life Science: Insect Metamorphosis.
Chapter 7: Visual Literacy in Earth Science: Phases of the Moon.
Chapter 8: Visual Literacy in Physical Science: Force and Motion.
Chapters 6, 7, and 8 are practice chapters. Each chapter provides the appropriate content standards from the *National Science Education Standards* (NRC 1996) for grades K–4 and 5–8 and several partial lessons that you can carry out in your classes or with your teammates if you are working in a professional learning community. Once you have practiced with your newly acquired methods of teaching visual literacy skills, we hope you will begin to integrate those methods into your science lessons.

Chapter 9: Visual Literacy: Next Steps. In this chapter we show that "being literate" is no longer limited to reading and writing. Literacy has come to include much more, including the ability to access, analyze, evaluate, and communicate in a variety of forms. Visual literacy includes both a process for learning and an expansion of the concept of text that includes visual images. Written text and visual images constitute the platform to help all students learn. By giving our "digital natives" visual literacy tools, we help them organize the information they need to learn and retain. This can be one of the greatest learning gifts science teachers provide for their students.

CHAPTER 1
Visual Literacy:
The Primer

Have you ever tried to assemble a child's toy or undertake a home repair without the aid of a picture, illustration, or diagram? Such tasks can be almost impossible if you do not have a "visual text" to help you interpret and make sense of the written instructions. In a reverse but equally frustrating situation, students often encounter visual texts for the first time and are expected to interpret their meaning and recognize their relevance. Classroom science programs need to provide students with explicit instructions in how to navigate these visuals, to interpret the information presented, and to make and use visuals as a means to demonstrate understanding. One of the great advantages of visual texts such as pictures, maps, diagrams, charts, and graphs is that they can be made accessible to all readers, including very young students who are not yet readers of words as well as students for whom English is not their first language.

The term *visual literacy* is credited to John Debes, cofounder of the International Visual Literacy Association, who in 1969 offered this definition:

> Visual literacy refers to a group of vision-competencies a human being can develop by seeing and at the same time having and integrating other sensory experiences. The development of these competencies is fundamental to normal human learning. When developed, they enable a visually literate person to discriminate and interpret the visible actions, objects, [and] symbols, natural or man-made, that he encounters in his environment. Through the creative use of these competencies, he is able to communicate with others. Through the appreciative use of these competencies, he is able to comprehend and enjoy the master-works of visual communication. (pp. 25–26)

Debes makes the case that "seeing" something is not the same as "viewing" something—that a person's ability to make sense of what is seen is infused with other inputs, both real (sound, touch, taste, and smell) and imagined (e.g., emotions, ideas). Altogether, these sensory inputs help a person interpret an image, derive meaning from it, and at the same time evaluate its importance or relevance. The term *visual literacy* is used in slightly different ways in different disciplines, such as education, art history and criticism, philosophy, information design, and graphic design. For the purpose of this book, we have a very simple definition: Visual literacy is the ability to (a) read and interpret a visual image and (b) communicate information using visual representations.

Using the See-Scan-Analyze Thinking Process

As a science educator, you are familiar with the science concepts and topics you teach. But suppose you were asked to think about a topic in a field with which you were not so familiar. Your students are often in that uncomfortable situation. Try to imagine your students struggling to understand an unfamiliar concept in an American history textbook. As they read a passage about, say, the impact of the automobile on American society, they grapple with trying to decode new vocabulary words. They also try to make sense of the expository nature of the text by deriving meaning from and understanding the

Figure 1.1 "Auto Wreck, USA, 1923"

Source: U.S. Library of Congress Prints and Photographs Division. Digital ID npcc.09083.

relevance of the material they are reading—doing all this, perhaps, without a clear mental vision of the topic's importance or purpose.

Undoubtedly some students will become disinterested, bored, or unmotivated. How might visual images help such students better understand the topic? Let's consider some possibilities. Try the following exercise. Look carefully at Figure 1.1 "Auto Wreck, USA, 1923" and then answer the questions.

- What did you think was happening in the photograph? How long did it take you to decide (30 seconds, a minute, maybe two minutes)? What information in the photograph helped you decide what was happening?
- Did you wonder why the people were gathered around the car?
- Were you curious to know how the car ended up this way?
- Did you wonder about when and where this scene took place?

Before you could decide what you thought was happening in the photograph, no doubt you had to look at it to gather information on which to base your conclusion. You had to stop for a minute to see what details the photograph contained. Scanning the picture gave you a sense of what you thought was happening, or what had already occurred. Your brain analyzed this incoming information from your eyes and, without effort, tried to organize it, make sense of it, and assign some importance to it. In other words, the image conveyed information that your eyes read and your mind processed in order to "make meaning."

Most viewers gather information quickly and almost effortlessly from a photograph such as this one, just as fluent readers do from written material. Fluent readers do not stop on each word as they are reading; instead, they scan the text and derive meaning from the combination of phrases and key words as they go. They pick only what they deem to be essential bits of information and string them together as they read. They derive meaning from the text, and only when the meaning becomes confused or unclear do they slow down or stop to reread. They reread to clarify or confirm what they thought they knew or to reassess their thinking with the addition of new information.

Figure 1.2 See-Scan-Analyze Thinking Process

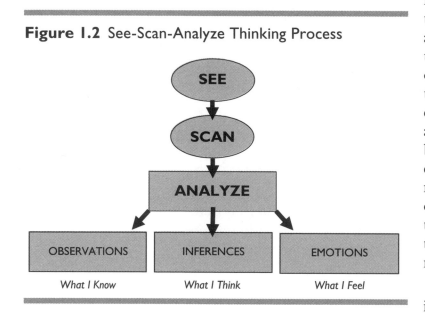

Good observers of visual images follow the same steps as fluent readers do. In the few seconds it took you to view the photograph in Figure 1.1, your eyes had scanned the photograph and gathered in the details. Your brain began to process that information, analyze it, and relate it to your own personal experiences. Your brain also assigned relevance or importance to the information, which together helped you arrive at some explanation. Almost without effort, what we call the see-scan-analyze thinking process (Figure 1.2) occurred, and you reached a conclusion about what you thought was happening in the photograph.

This see-scan-analyze thinking processing of information is automatic. Each phase of the process occurs quickly and without cognitive effort. The one exception is in the case of young children, who do not intuitively move through the phase of assigning significance to the viewing process. Teachers must help them develop the ability to reflect metacognitively (i.e., think about what they are viewing and have a mental discourse about its relevance) so that they can become visually literate. Just as in reading, children need explicit instruction and guidance in developing the ability to critically analyze what they see. They need to be encouraged to make observations, ask themselves questions about what they see, take time to reflect on what they saw, and then be shown how to put that information together. A teacher's guiding questions can help students recognize that visual images can be essential tools to assist them in their understanding of a science concept (see pp. 67, 69–70, 88–89, 90–91, 104, 106, and 108 for samples of questions that will engage your students with the content of the lesson).

Mind, Brain, and Patterns for Learning

Current brain research has provided many insights into how the brain unconsciously takes in and consciously processes information. As Pat Wolfe, a leader in translating brain research for practitioners, has written, "Neuroscientists tell us that the brain organizes information in networks and maps" (Wolfe 2004, as cited in Hyerle 2009, p. 2). Hyerle (2009) further notes that "the brain, we have come to understand, is an organism that has a specialized, continuously evolving, multidimensional, and dynamic *spatial* architecture that networks and maps information" (p. 2).

For learners to take full advantage of this dynamic process, they must be able to pay attention, process information, build meaning, store and recall information, and then extend this new information to new situations. Fortunately, our brains are up to the task!

Remarkably, unbelievably, the brain is capable of absorbing 36,000 visual images every hour. How can this imponderable ability be true? It is because the sophisticated visual capacity of our brain system is beyond the conscious processing of our mind: research approximates that between 70 and 90% of the information received by the brain is through visual channels. Though our auditory and kinesthetic modes of "sensing" are complex, the brain's *dominant* and most efficiently sensory filter for most information is our eyes. (Hyerle 2009, pp. 28–29)

Effective educators understand how students can become better visual learners. These teachers (a) provide students with explicit instruction on interpreting visuals (e.g., pp. 2–5 on the see-scan-analyze thinking process) and (b) show them how to create their own visual representations to help them remember what they read, hear, see, and experience (see, especially, Chapter 5).

Learning combines information with understanding in an organized framework. Viewing a visual image follows the same systemic functions that one uses when reading a work of fiction or nonfiction. The viewer or reader "constructs" three types of meaning simultaneously: the ideas or the context of the text; the content or information written about or depicted in the text; and the text's interpersonal significance, which is the nature of the relationship between the viewer and the text. Think back to the photograph "Auto Wreck" (p. 3). As a viewer looking at the photograph for the first time, your brain is instantly processing the information it is receiving from your eyes and trying to derive meaning from it. As this sensory input streams in, your brain is working to answer three questions simultaneously: What is the purpose of this picture? What are the details within the picture? What is the relevance of this picture to me?

This information processing occurs automatically and effortlessly without any intentional or purposeful mental effort. In other words, the brain is trying to sift through the sensory input and develop "answers" to those three questions, which are, to phrase them a little differently, What does this picture mean or for what purpose am I viewing it? How do the details within the picture support what it means? Is this picture relevant to me (either as in "why should I care?" or "why must I know this?") or does it tap into my emotions and spark a feeling response (such as "I sympathize with someone who has a disabled car")?

In the case of "Auto Wreck," the viewer may be comparing historical time periods and considering the impact of the automobile on 19th-century American culture (context). The details of the picture with the broken wheel and the group of men standing around the automobile support the idea that the automobile was a novelty among most Americans, with the broken wheel signifying that the repair process will not be an easy one (content). A viewer's interpersonal connections can cover a wide range of possible scenarios and are dependent on the observer's experiences and mood. A possible interpersonal reaction might be a feeling of connection because the viewer has had an auto wreck with a flat tire. The photograph might be relevant to the viewer because he or she has had experiences with that model of automobile or because he or she recognizes the locale where the photograph was taken (which happens to be in Washington, D.C., in front of what was then known as the Library of Congress Building).

As the brain processes this information, the brain must decide what to do with the information that has been received. It must connect what it has viewed with something it is already familiar with in order to store and later retrieve this information. This process of the construction of meaning is explained in *How People Learn: Brain, Mind, Experience, and School*: "To develop competence in an area of inquiry, students must (a) have a deep foundation of factual knowledge, (b) understand facts and ideas in the context of a conceptual framework, and (c) organize knowledge in ways that facilitate retrieval and application" (Bransford, Brown, and Cocking 2000, p. 16). For students to derive meaning, learning must combine information with conceptual understanding in an organized framework. This does not mean that hands-on or inquiry-based activities are not necessary in the learning process. Instead it means that in the development of conceptual understanding, students must acquire (or construct) a foundation of factual knowledge that is in some way organized and readily accessible to them. It is in this aspect of learning that it is critical that students are able to read visual images and create thinking tools, such as concept maps and graphic organizers.

Creating a Visual Tool for Long-Term Learning

Let's now consider two different types of visuals and graphic organizers that might be used in a science lesson: the popular Venn diagram and the three-dimensional graphic organizer. Please keep in mind that we are not providing complete lessons here or in the content chapters, 6–8.*

We will look at the subject of cells, a subject found in most intermediate and middle grades curricula. Understanding that cells are the basic building blocks of all living things is crucial to later understanding more complex biological concepts, as expressed in *National Science Education Standards* (NRC 1996), Content Standard C, Structure and Function in Living Systems, 5–8:

> Living systems at all levels of organization demonstrate the complementary nature of structure and function. Important levels of organization for structure and function include cells, organs, tissues, organ systems, whole organisms, and ecosystems. (p. 156)

Give students the following instructions: *Read the information in Figure 1.3. As you are reading, you should be thinking about how you are taking in the information, mentally organizing it, and making meaning from it. Then answer the questions at the end of the figure.*

(Some teachers—and maybe some students—will be very familiar with the information presented here. The point of this exercise is not to teach students about cells but rather to have them begin to develop an awareness of the relationship between text and visual images.)

According to the dual-coding theory of information storage (Paivio 1991), information is processed and stored in memory in two forms: a linguistic form (words or statements) and a nonlinguistic visual form (mental pictures or physical sensations). We now know that the way knowledge is coded in the brain has

---

*In Chapters 6–8, we provide opportunities for teachers to practice creating questions related to science lesson visuals. These chapters can be used in professional development settings or in professional learning communities in which teachers can read and discuss each section. Each of these chapters focuses on a different strand of science—insect metamorphosis (life science), phases of the Moon (Earth science), and force and motion (physical science). The examples are from different grade spans based on the National Science Education Standards (NRC 1996). We encourage collaborative discussion as a way to further develop one's own visual literacy skills.

Figure 1.3 Plant and Animal Cells: How Do They Compare?

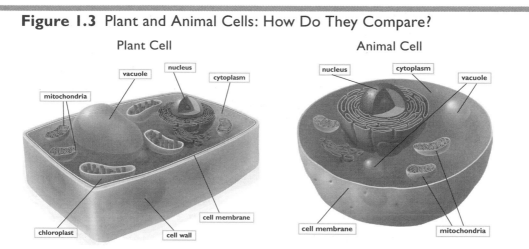

Source: Hackett, J. K., R. H. Moyer, and J. Vasquez. 2008. *Science A Closer Look.* Grade 5, Visual Literacy. Columbus, OH: Macmillan/McGraw-Hill, pp. 2, 24. Copyright © 2008 Macmillan/McGraw-Hill. Reprinted with permission.

All cells have smaller parts that help them stay alive. But all cells are not the same. Although plant cells and animal cells have some of the same cell parts, plant cells have some things that animal cells do not have.

Most plant cells have green parts called *chloroplasts.* Chloroplasts are filled with a green substance called *chlorophyll.* This substance helps plants make food using the Sun's energy. The chloroplast is often called the plant's food factory.

Plant cells also have sturdy *cell walls.* Cell walls give the plant cell a shape like a box and help protect and support the cell. Animal cells have a *cell membrane,* but they do not have cell walls. The cell membrane is a thin covering found on the outside of the animal cell. In plants, the cell membrane is inside the cell wall.

Both plant and animal cells have *mitochondria.* In the mitochondria food is burned to give the cell its energy. Both plant and animal cells also have a *nucleus,* which controls all cell activities, and *chromosomes,* which control how the cell develops. Both plant and animal cells have *vacuoles,* which are structures in which the cell's food, water, and wastes are stored. Plant cells have one or two *vacuoles.* Animal cells have many more. And both plant and animal cells have *cytoplasm.* This substance that fills the cell is mostly water and has important chemicals for the cells.

After reading the above, think about—or talk with a partner about—the following questions:

- How did you process the information that you just read?

- Did you examine each diagram individually before you read the text?

- Did you read the text first and then examine each diagram?

- Did you quickly scan the diagrams, recognize what they represented, and then move down to see what information the text provided?

- As you were reading the text did you go back and confirm what you were reading by looking at the diagrams?

- Did the diagrams help to clarify the information presented in words?

significant implications for teaching—and particularly for the way we help students acquire and retain knowledge. As Marzano, Pickering, and Pollock (2001) point out, "The primary way we present new knowledge to students is linguistic. We either talk to them about the new content or have them read about it" (p. 73). The fact that education gives so much weight to the verbal processing of knowledge means that students are often left on their own to interpret visuals and are rarely given the opportunity to create their own visual representations. By actually creating a visual "model"—a visual thinking tool—students can become active participants in their learning as opposed to being passive receivers. In the case of the plant and animal cells, students might use a thinking tool such as a Venn diagram to compare and contrast the two types of cells (Figure 1.4).

Figure 1.4 Venn Diagram: How are plant and animal cells alike and different? (Compare/Contrast Graphic Organizer)

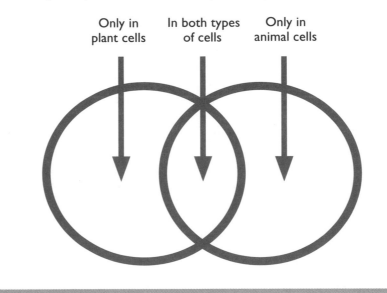

An even more interactive method than the Venn diagram to help students visualize and recall new information is the three-dimensional graphic organizer, often called a foldable. (See Chapter 5 for greater detail on the use of foldables.) This type

Figure 1.5 Animal Cell (Shutter-Fold Graphic Organizer; opens in the middle)

Figure 1.6 Plant Cell (Shutter-Fold Graphic Organizer; opens at the top and bottom)

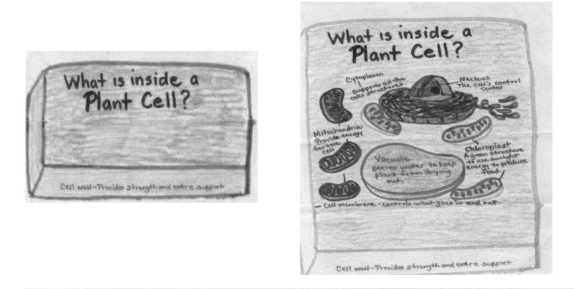

The foldables on this page were constructed for use in this book by Frankie Troutman, a veteran elementary school teacher and one of the authors of the book. These visual literacy tools are normally constructed in the classroom by students.

of organizer is student-created and can actually demonstrate what students are thinking. Figure 1.5 (p. 11) is a representation of an animal cell in a "shutter-fold" graphic organizer that opens in the middle. Figure 1.6 (p. 11) is a representation of a plant cell in a shutter-fold graphic organizer that opens at the top and bottom.

As students try out such visual literacy tools, they will begin to "see" concepts and build relationships among ideas by layering new information onto existing knowledge. These powerful tools can be easily integrated into a teacher's regular instructional practices. They can also help teachers assess their students' conceptual understandings and identify their misconceptions. And, once students themselves are familiar with the idea and the process of creating different types of visual tools, they will begin to incorporate them naturally into their learning routines.

Summary

> The brain is sometimes referred to as a sponge that soaks up information. Perhaps a more accurate metaphor would be a sieve, because by some estimates, 99 percent of all sensory information is discarded almost immediately upon entering the brain. (Gazzaniga 1998, p. 79)

Teachers often give students more information than they can possibly assimilate. Without some mechanism for organizing this raw sensory data into meaningful patterns, most of it is discarded (or else learned for the test and then filtered out of the brain forever). Visual literacy tools can be powerful teaching allies in helping students process, organize, interpret, and apply the information they need to know and understand to be successful in the science classroom.

CHAPTER 2
Interpreting Photographs

> "A picture shows me at a glance what it takes dozens of pages in a book to expound."
>
> —Ivan Turgenev, *Fathers and Sons* (1862)

A single graphic image can capture the meaning of a complex idea or concept that would require many pages of text to describe. A photograph, in particular, can sometimes tell a story far more easily than can many pages of narration. Take the photograph in Figure 2.1 (p. 14), for example. Suppose you were to ask your students (before showing them the photograph) this thought-provoking question: "What do you think a jungle looks like to a person riding on the back of an elephant?"

What might they say? How would they describe this experience? Probably most of them have seen an elephant, but few would have had the chance to ride on one. They could probably describe the elephant and the jungle, but not the view from the elephant's back. Then show them the picture in Figure 2.1. To heighten your students' awareness of the many elements in this photograph, you might ask them these questions:

- What is the position of the viewer in this picture?
- Where is the rest of the elephant?
- As we study the picture, what senses in addition to our sight might come into play?

- What does the vegetation indicate?
- What might it feel like to touch the elephant's head? Do you think it is it smooth and leathery? Or would the hairs make it prickly?

Some of these questions can be answered by direct observation. Others require inferences drawn from these observations. For example, we might say it is a sunny day. We *infer* the Sun is shining because of the brightness of the photograph and the shadows cast by the trees. Students may have seen the Disney movie *The Jungle Book* (1967) and some even may have read Kipling's collection of stories called *The Jungle Book* (1894). How would seeing the photograph enhance their understanding of the movie or the stories? The point of this exercise is to help students begin to establish a three-step routine when they look at photographs: make observations, draw inferences, and ask questions as they work to gather information.

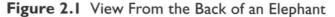

Figure 2.1 View From the Back of an Elephant

Source: SXC.hu, HAAP Media Ltd.

Metacognition and Graphic Images

The ability to absorb and interpret information is the hallmark of a visually literate person. Visual learning—the process by which people become visually literate—links visual literacy with constructivist learning through the role of each in acquiring knowledge. When by *visual literacy* we mean the ability of individuals to discriminate, interpret, and construct meaning from the *images* they encounter, we see that these experiences are very like the experiences students have when they build knowledge from their interactions with their *physical environments*. Both kinds of experiences provide students with the opportunity to create meaning based on their personal interactions. As Stokes (2002) points out, "Technology, particularly the graphical user interface of the World Wide Web, requires reading and writing skills to be applied in a visual context in order to derive meaning from what is being communicated" (p. 10).

Student textbooks today provide a wealth of pictures and illustrations to make learning easier. The internet has opened the door to an unlimited source of images that teachers can use in the classroom, in PowerPoint presentations, and in interactive whiteboard applications. This use of images can provide students with a vast array of experiences and a wealth of examples to facilitate their learning.

Yet, at the same time, students can find this abundance of images complicating and confusing. If students don't have strategies for accessing the information locked inside the images, the images turn into obstacles that impede learning. Teachers cannot assume that children will recognize the relevance of the images they view or that children will connect the importance of the images to their learning. Comprehension of new images—particularly those that are outside the range of images of "everyday," familiar things and scenes—requires special knowledge and skills. Teachers must engage in specific learning activities that help their students develop the skills and knowledge necessary to make meaning from the images they view and *then* relate the meaning to the science content they are studying.

Teachers often assume that photographs are easy for students to understand, requiring little skill on the students' part and minimal instruction from the teacher. As a teacher, you even might be tempted to say to yourself, *That image speaks for itself. My students just need to look at it to know what they are looking at.*

In fact, as we have discussed, *looking* at an image is only the first step in a much more complex process. Visually literate persons should be able to ask themselves questions that will help them appreciate the meaning of what they are looking at and evaluate the importance and relevance of a visual image. This metacognitive approach to looking at images helps students be actively engaged in the process of learning.

To be visually literate, students need to

- recognize the importance that pictures play in conveying scientific information,
- know when to pause and carefully analyze pictures, and
- learn about when and where the pictures are relevant and how they can use these pictures in their learning.

Older students also need to recognize the difference between pictures in textbooks and the commercial advertisements on their social network pages.

Actively Promoting Visual Literacy

Students with limited concept knowledge may regard certain visual images as presenting them with excessive complexities and incomprehensible information if the connections to the concepts are not obvious to them (Chanlin 1997). Teachers, therefore, need to actively promote instructional strategies to assist all learners to make connections between the text and the visuals. Using Figure 2.2 as a reference for your thinking, try the following exercise with the photograph in Figure 2.3:

1. Write three headings on a piece of paper: "Observations," "Inferences," and "Emotions."

2. Under the heading "Observations," make a list of what you actually see in the photograph. Use phrases or sentences.

Figure 2.2 See-Scan-Analyze Thinking Process

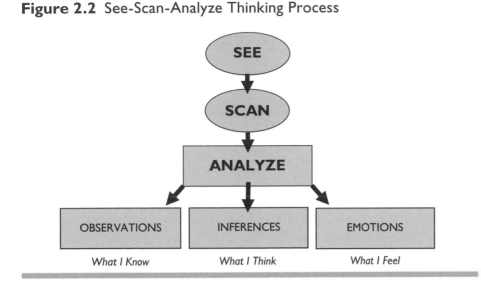

3. Under the heading "Inferences," make a list of what assumptions you can make or conclusions you can draw based on your observations. (If you are doing this activity with young children, the words *inference* and *assumption* will probably be too advanced. Instead, perhaps use "my best guess.")

4. Under the heading "Emotions," make a list of the feelings the picture evokes for you.

   Did your lists include some of these statements?

Observations

- There is a child.
- The child is sitting in the grass.
- The child is looking away to the left from the viewer's perspective.
- The child is wearing shorts.
- The child has short hair.
- There is a bandage on the child's wrist.
- The child is missing some teeth.
- There is a dog.
- The dog is black.
- The dog is looking away from the photographer.

Figure 2.3 Child and Dog

Source: SXC.hu, HAAP Media Ltd.

Inferences

- The child is a boy.
- The child is around six or seven years old.
- The weather is warm.
- The grass is green.
- The dog is a puppy.
- Someone is talking to the boy.
- The boy has petted puppies before.
- The picture was taken outdoors.

Emotions

If you do this activity as a class with your students, the list of emotions will probably be very long. That is because each viewer's own perceptions and experiences will color his or her interpretations. For example, a student may be allergic to dogs, and so that child's emotions might include fear ("I'm allergic to dogs and I would never pet it"). Other emotions among children might include worry ("I would like to pet the puppy, but I'd have to be sure to wash my hands afterward") and empathy ("I bet the boy really enjoys petting the dog, and I would like to pet the dog, too").

Here are some other possible observations and inferences you or a class might have:

Observation: A child is sitting and petting a dog. The child is smiling.

Inference: Based on the position of the smiling child sitting on the ground and touching the dog, the child is happy. The dog is small in size so we assume it is a puppy.

Observation: The child is looking away from the photographer. The dog is looking in the same direction as the boy.

Inference: Off to the side, out of the view of the camera, something is attracting their attention. It appears that the action they are looking at is pleasant because both are attentive and do not appear alarmed.

Observation: There is a bandage on the child's arm.

Inference: The child had some cut or injury that required a bandage.

The photograph in Figure 2.3 was taken from an elementary science lesson in which students viewed a series of photographs illustrating different stages of growth and development in mammals. This particular photograph allowed students to make conjectures and to create "what-if" scenarios about the subjects in the photograph. Thus, students were using the science skill of inquiry via observation—just as real scientists do. After all, as science teachers know, the inquiry nature of science is not limited to doing an activity or investigation; it includes making careful observations. In the real world, scientists ask themselves questions about what they have observed. They then speculate or hypothesize about possible or plausible reasons for why something has happened. When a teacher and the class take time to analyze a photograph, the teacher is modeling the behavior of scientists and supporting the goals of scientific inquiry.

Fostering Questions and Curiosity

Our observations of the photo "Child and Dog" have provided a list of factual evidence. By analyzing those facts, we can arrive at some reasonable explanations. However, not all of our questions can be answered by our observations and the inferences we made. Look at the photograph once more. What other questions do you still have—and might your students also have—about the picture? For example, did you wonder if the child just got the dog or what type of breed the dog is? Are there other puppies nearby that are not in the picture? Is this a recent picture or one taken some time ago? Was this a professionally staged photograph?

Such questions arise from our sense of curiosity and wonder. Because we do not have any additional information that can help us answer them, we are left to speculate. This type of speculation is healthy for students. It allows them to freely express their thinking. There are no wrong answers to any of the above questions because we do not have any factual information to validate or dispute any answers our students propose. Such speculation can lead to creative learning opportunities, such as writing a story about what might have happened just before the picture was taken or about what might happen next. Students can pretend to be the child in the photograph and create a dialogue with the puppy. The photograph can be used as a tool to encourage students to write more descriptively than they have in the past, write from different perspectives, or write a narrative (a story).

Our interest and motivation will determine how closely we examine the details of a photograph. Consider, for example, a photograph of a movie star in a magazine and a photomicrograph of a diamond crystal in a science journal. On one hand, if we are more interested in the movie star than in the diamond crystal, we may analyze the magazine picture to gather information and to satisfy our curiosity. We may be curious to see what the movie star is wearing or maybe who else is in the picture. We may want to know where the movie star has been or where she or he was when the picture was taken. On the other hand, if we are more interested in the diamond crystal, we may be intrigued by the crystalline structure of the mineral, the details in the high resolution of the shot, or the process through which the image was captured. In either case, however, we view that image with the same see-scan-analyze thinking process (Figure 2.2) as we did the picture of the elephant. Our interest and curiosity prompt us to examine and evaluate the image before us.

When students are reading science textbooks and reference materials, teachers need to remind them that the pictures provided are purposeful and not just decorations or distractions placed there to interfere with their learning. They are valuable visual tools that can help students make sense of the words on the page and build understanding of the concepts being presented.

In today's society, where images are flashed at us constantly, neither we nor our students can take the time, or make the mental effort, to analyze all those images individually. We become immune to the importance that pictures can have, and therefore their importance is diminished. However, we can help our students recognize that pictures—in reference resources, picture guides, textbooks, and online research articles—relate useful and valuable information. We can also help them develop the internal see-scan-analyze thinking process. Students must unlock information in a picture and recognize how to use it.

CHAPTER 3
Interpreting Diagrams

Did you know you could read Arabic? Look at the diagram in Figure 3.1 (p. 22), which was taken from an Arabic language science textbook. Without knowing the language or being able to read the text, can you figure out what information is being conveyed? Although you probably guessed that the diagram was identifying the parts of the plant, you did not need to read Arabic in order to decipher that meaning.

Think for a minute about what mental processes you used to "unlock" or "decode" the information pictured. Initially, you probably recognized the image as a plant by its general structure and specifically as a strawberry plant because of the characteristic shape of the fruit. As you looked at the diagram, did you scan or survey the entire image? You probably recognized that the labels were pointing to specific features of the plant. You also probably recognized that the view of the roots was different from the rest of the image. The cutaway section of the drawing below ground level allowed for an "inside" view of the structures that are normally hidden from view below the soil.

Making such mental assessments about what a diagram or other image is depicting can come naturally after repeated exposures. Some students, however, do not make the mental assessments you probably made because they lack practice or experience in analyzing the information in an image.

The Challenge of Complicated Images

In today's society, we are constantly bombarded with pictures and images. Sometimes those images are easy to understand. For example, consider the use of international travel symbols. In any public place around the world, various universally accepted symbols are used to denote things such as restrooms, restaurants, sleeping accommodations, or information services. These visual symbols simplify the task of conveying fundamental information without the need for multiple translations. The symbols reflect very basic human needs that are related to our daily activities.

In areas of study such as science and technology, however, the kind of information being conveyed in pictures and images is more specialized and technical. It is information we normally do not come in contact with in the course of our everyday experiences. Analyzing and interpreting visual presentations of scientific and technical information requires additional cognitive effort if we are to make sense of it and to recognize its importance.

Look now at Figure 3.2. It too is from an Arabic language science textbook. Unlike the diagram of the strawberry plant in Figure 3.1, however, the diagram in Figure 3.2 includes a variety of illustrative techniques that can make the transfer of information more complicated. For example, in addition to labels for certain features, the graphic designer has used captions, cutaways, and close-ups.

Figure 3.1 Strawberry Plant (Text in Arabic)

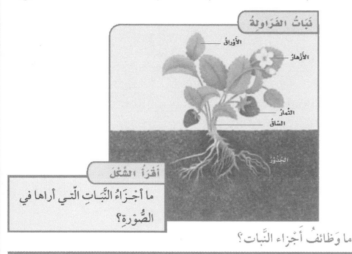

Source: Hackett, J. K., R. H. Moyer, and J. Vasquez. 2008. *Science A Closer Look.* Columbus, OH: Macmillan/McGraw-Hill/Obeikan Research and Development. Copyright © 2008 Macmillan/McGraw-Hill. Reprinted with permission.

Think about how you read this diagram. What information is it depicting? Reflect on how you mentally processed the structure of the diagram and how you analyzed the structure in order to gather the information. Also consider these questions:

- Did you recognize that the circles to the left of the boy represented the ever-increasing magnification of the heart muscle tissue? How did you know that? What clues in the illustration helped you know that?
- Did the order or placement of the circles in the diagram support your understanding of that relationship?

Figure 3.2 Example of the Organization of a System (Text in Arabic)

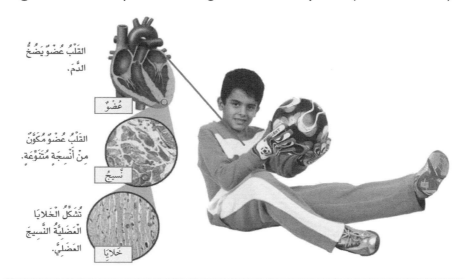

Source: Hackett, J. K., R. H. Moyer, and J. Vasquez. 2008. *Science A Closer Look.* Columbus, OH: Macmillan/ McGraw-Hill/Obeikan Research and Development. Copyright © 2008 Macmillan/McGraw-Hill. Reprinted with permission.

You probably noted correctly that the diagram illustrates the complex organization of a human body system, in this case part of the circulatory system. The sequence of images on the left depicts the organizational levels: from the top, organ (heart), tissue (muscle), cells (cardiac muscle cells). The placement of the circles helps the viewer "get" the descending, hierarchical order of the images. It also implies that the circles depict some sort of

CHAPTER 3

relationship to one another. Certainly the text accompanying the diagram did not offer you any clues to the information that was being conveyed (unless, of course, you read Arabic).

Teachers should be aware that students who are not aware of the illustrative technique of using insets might misinterpret the relative size (or scale*) in the relationship between each of the circles. They might inaccurately assume that the heart, tissue, and cells are all the same size. Teachers might need to instruct students to compare the size of the heart to the size of the boy, then look at the sequence of insets showing the heart wall, the heart tissue from the heart wall, and the strands of cardiac muscle cells from the heart tissue. The teacher may need to point out that each insert represents a magnified view of the preceding image.

Inner Conversations When Viewing a Diagram

In each of the figures, you, as the viewer of the image, had to read the picture. As you looked at each diagram, you made mental assessments and "constructed" meaning as you were decoding the details of the image. You probably drew on your past experiences or familiarity with the subject matter, making use of your prior knowledge. For example, your knowledge of plants probably helped you recognize that the diagram in Figure 3.1 was pointing out the plant parts, just as your knowledge of the heart helped you understand the purpose of the insets in Figure 3.2.

This process is similar to the way in which readers must carefully analyze written information. Readers relate what they read to what they know and what they have experienced in order to make sense of what they are reading. The "reader writes the story" (Harvey and Goudvis 2000). "An inner conversation takes place in the reader's mind that is unique to him or her—just as that person draws from a unique set of prior experiences or background knowledge…. We construct meaning based on the building of connections between our own personal schema and the new information" (Douglas, Klentschy, and Worth 2006, p. 129).

---

* The concept of scale will be new to some students, and it may be particularly challenging to those in grades K–4. Teachers might simply tell students that a "scale drawing [is one in which] a figure in the drawing is either enlarged or reduced in size from its original size" (Wisconsin State Superintendent of Public Instruction 2009). Teachers should be clear with students that when they use the word *scale* in the context of diagrams they are not referring to a bathroom scale, the scales on a fish, scaling a mountain, or measurement scales such the Richter scale. For an excellent collection of articles for middle school teachers on the subject of scale, see the December 2009 issue of the NSTA member journal *Science Scope* (*www.nsta.org/middleschool*). Teachers of younger students might find it helpful to read Moore, Dixon, and Haines (1991), Koellner-Clark (2003), and Larson (2009).

As you viewed the images in Figures 3.1 and 3.2, did you have that "inner conversation" in your mind? Perhaps you asked yourself questions such as these:

- What am I seeing?
- What does this image remind me of that I already know?
- Have I seen this image or something like it before?
- What is this illustration trying to show me? What is its purpose?

Like a good reader, a viewer who is unlocking the meaning of an illustration must be cognitively alert and actively engaged. Viewers must make the connection between what they know from their own experiences and what new information is being conveyed. It is important to help students become aware of this mental process and also be aware that different types of illustrative techniques can convey information differently.

To better understand difficulties that students can have with decoding information presented in illustrations, let us consider the purpose of illustrations. In general, illustrations are pictures that help make something clear or attractive. An illustration might be used to embellish a story, poem, or magazine article or to elucidate complex information, such as that found in a technical article or other sophisticated expository text. In science textbooks, illustrations show objects described in the text. They can help the viewer visualize step-by-step instructions in technical manuals, and they can depict subjects that are not visible to the human eye.

Diagrams, a form of illustration, tend to be drawings, sketches, or plans that help make something easier to understand; they explain how something works or describe the relationship between an object and its parts. Diagrams can be very simple or highly complex. Different types of diagrams serve different purposes when conveying information. Each type requires different skills for analysis, requiring viewers to ask themselves different types of questions as they work to unlock the meaning embedded within the diagram.

Making the transition from interpreting photographs to interpreting diagrams is an important step for students on the road to visual literacy. They first need to recognize how photographs differ from diagrams.

Photographs show us the "real thing." They reflect the surface textures, colors, and setting of the subject. Diagrams, however, require the viewer to interpret and reconstruct the general or characteristic features of the subject. Photographs are usually about the individual subject's unique characteristics or traits whereas diagrams make generalizations that define those "typical" characteristics.... (Moline 1995, p. 36)

Although diagrams allow for the addition of features that make them better than photographs for conveying major science concepts, the labels, arrows, and insets often used in diagrams—to show, perhaps, the motion of objects or the sequence of ongoing processes—add a layer of complexity for the viewer. Different types of questions are needed. As students work to interpret diagrams, they need to be aware of certain questions to ask themselves. Let us examine different types of diagrams and consider questioning strategies for each type. It is important that students be able to recognize that different types of diagrams convey information in unique ways. Eventually, students should be able to recognize—and perhaps even memorize the names of—several different types of diagrams.

Analytic Diagrams

Analytic diagrams, also known as simple diagrams, can be thought of as pictures with labels or captions. Generally, labels are just a few words; captions contain more detailed information. Most simple diagrams are used to define an object or a concept visually. Think of the diagram of the strawberry plant in Figure 3.1. It captures the concept that plants have specific parts and that those parts are located in specific places.

Sometimes an analytic diagram can be used to show the relationship between an object and its parts or to compare the size of the object with something familiar to the viewer (thereby providing a "context" for the labeled drawing). In the strawberry plant diagram (Figure 3.1), for example, the size of the plant and its parts all appear to be in proportion to one another. In the diagram showing the organization of the body system (Figure 3.2), the boy holding a soccer ball is recognizable and familiar to students and provides the "setting" for the placement of the parts of the body system. However, it should be noted that the size of the heart is not in proportion to the size of the boy's body.

Analytic diagrams can also help define categories or classify items into groups or subgroups. These types of diagrams are very powerful tools because they help students define or explain concepts that are hard to describe in words or that require multiple pages of text to describe. For example, look at another diagram of the parts of the strawberry plant, this time with the labels in English (Figure 3.3). Each part of the plant is labeled and is clearly depicted in its appropriate position in relation to the other parts of the plant. The size of each part is in proportion relative to the size of all the other parts of the plant. The details of the strawberry plant are accurate and realistic.

What makes this diagram distinctive, however, is that it, like the diagram in Figure 3.1, uses a *cutaway view* to show what is beneath the soil. The purpose of the cutaway technique is to highlight or "unveil" a view of something that is not normally seen. In this case, the roots of the plant are shown in the cutaway. (It is important to mention to students that although the cutaway technique is showing what is beneath the ground, the diagram does not include the internal structures of the whole plant above the ground.) If you ask your students to describe why the cutaway view is useful, you are helping them recognize the purpose of this illustrative technique.

The diagram of the ocean floor (Figure 3.4, p. 28) is similar in its construction to the diagram of the strawberry plant. Labels with lines indicate and identify specific features. The cutaway view below the surface of the water, like the cutaway in Figure 3.3, shows features that are normally out of view. What may not be evident to students is that *unlike* the diagram in Figure 3.3, the features in Figure 3.4 are not drawn to scale (in the diagram, the objects do not have the same size and shape relationships to one

Figure 3.3 Strawberry Plant (Labels in English)

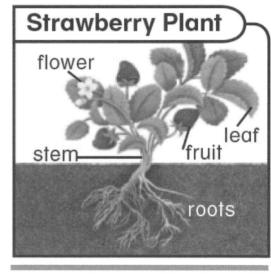

Source: Hackett, J. K., R. H. Moyer, and J. Vasquez. 2008. *Science A Closer Look.* Grade 1, Visual Literacy. Columbus, OH: Macmillan/McGraw-Hill, p. 32. Copyright © 2008 Macmillan/McGraw-Hill. Reprinted with permission.

another that they would have in real life). This diagram is simply meant to convey an understanding of features of the ocean floor. It also highlights key vocabulary. It does not realistically depict the relative size or position of the identified features. In other words, students should recognize that although simple diagrams can convey a great deal of useful information—for example, new vocabulary words and major ideas—distortions of scale (in respect to comparative size or spacing) and/or proportion can exist in simple diagrams.

Figure 3.4 The Ocean Floor

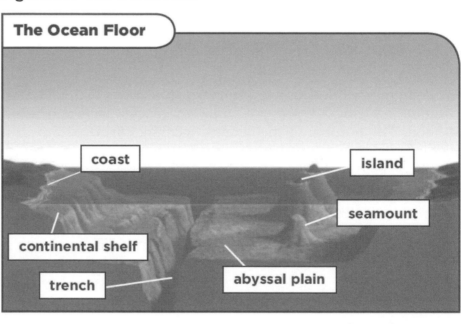

Source: Hackett, J. K., R. H. Moyer, and J. Vasquez. 2008. *Science A Closer Look.* Grade 3, Visual Literacy. Columbus, OH: Macmillan/McGraw-Hill, p. 28. Copyright © 2008 Macmillan/McGraw-Hill. Reprinted with permission.

Most students are familiar with the format of a labeled diagram. They can easily recognize its purpose as a means of locating and defining the parts or features of the object depicted. They understand that the labels can be read in any order since their placement does not interfere with the meaning attached to them and that a cutaway view (e.g., the plant roots and the ocean floor) depict what would normally be hidden from view. When you help students analyze the information in simple diagrams, you should ask them to ask themselves the following questions:

- Are there any words in this diagram that are new to me or that I've seen before but don't understand? (Example: the term *seamount* in Figure 3.4)
- How does the diagram help me organize or categorize information? (Example: the parts of a plant in Figure 3.3)
- Does the diagram show me how the parts of the object fit together or how they are related to one another? (Example: the organization, location, and arrangement of the parts of the plant in Figure 3.3)
- Does the diagram show me something that a person would not usually be able to see? (Example: the cutaway technique identifies the underground roots of the strawberry plant in Figure 3.1 and Figure 3.3 and the elements of the ocean floor in Figure 3.4)
- Does the diagram depict the actual size of the object or the relative size of its features (as in Figure 3.3) or does it not contain any information about proportional size relationships (as in Figure 3.4)?

These types of inquiry questions help students become more aware of the details in a diagram and how important these details can be to understanding the information in the text. The illustrative techniques used to relate the information depend on the purpose of the diagram.

Synthetic Diagrams

Synthetic diagrams can be described as illustrations that show connections between parts of a sequence or that link subgroups together within a larger group. Synthetic diagrams often use arrows or numbers to make the connections apparent to the viewer. They include flow charts, classification trees, and concept webs. They may be used to explain or summarize a process that moves through time or space (e.g., the water cycle), demonstrate growth or change (e.g., the life cycle of a pine tree), identify cause and effect (e.g., the action of a force upon an object), or present a series of steps or instructions (e.g., a wastewater treatment process). There are multiple formats for synthetic diagrams, which can range from simple linear-flow diagrams that usually contain pictures to more complex, multipage tree or web diagrams that may contain only text.

As in simple analytic diagrams, certain visual techniques are used in synthetic diagrams to convey highly conceptual information. Simple synthetic diagrams are straightforward and usually exhibit directionality. The simplest form is a sequence of images joined together with arrows (e.g., Figure 3.5); the images are usually read from left to right or top to bottom (or sometimes bottom to top). Synthetic diagrams require a minimum of cognitive effort for students because they mimic the linguistic format familiar to most students as they learn to read. (Of course, not all students may be familiar with that format because not all languages follow the left to right and top to bottom orientation.)

Figures 3.5, 3.6, 3.7, and 3.8 (pp. 31–35) show four different types of synthetic diagrams. After viewing each one, think about the mental processes you used to interpret it.

Linear Diagrams

Linear diagrams can get long and complex, linking multiple pictures that may take up several lines (called chain diagrams) or presenting viewers with several optional paths off the main route to follow and allowing them to retrace their paths and choose different paths (called tree diagrams).

Chain Diagrams

Look closely at Figure 3.5, a type of linear diagram of a pond food chain. Then, consider this question: Did you start with the title? If so, did reading the title make it easier to identify what information the diagram was conveying?

The arrows between the images appear to link each picture together. The sequence of images in this diagram seems to indicate that there is an order or progression that moves across the entire diagram from one box to another. The placement and orientation of the arrows provides directionality in viewing, encouraging the viewer to begin at the left. The text in the captions below each picture helps clarify or explain the purpose of each picture. But what do the arrows represent? In Figure 3.5 the arrows represent the flow of energy moving across the food chain. Some students may confuse the organization and sequence as depicting the food source for each organism and miss the key concept: the energy flow through the food chain.

In Figure 3.5, there is a blend of artistic drawing and real photographs. Does that technique make it easier to analyze or does it present another layer of complexity for the viewer? In interpreting simple linear diagrams, it is important that students recognize where the process begins and what significance the arrows have that link the images together.

Figure 3.5 Pond Food Chain (Chain Diagram)

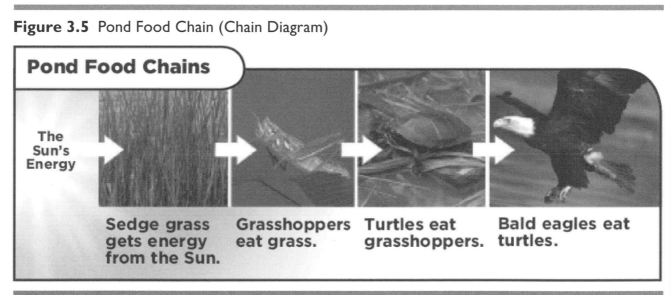

Source: Hackett, J. K., R. H. Moyer, and J. Vasquez. 2008. *Science A Closer Look.* Grade 3, Visual Literacy. Columbus, OH: Macmillan/McGraw-Hill, p. 15. Copyright © 2008 Macmillan/McGraw-Hill. Reprinted with permission.

Tree Diagrams

Tree diagrams take the form of tree branches that connect objects or concepts in a series of forked paths. They are useful for classifying groups and subgroups or for organizing information in hierarchies. They are organized with the major (dominant) idea at the starting position and with the lesser (supportive) details flowing from it. Whether the tree is built top down or bottom up, each limb or branch can be traced from the major idea or topic. The information can be read in either direction as the flow generally does not depict a process but rather demonstrates organizational relationships.

Figure 3.6 Pedigree Diagram for Dimples (Tree Diagram)

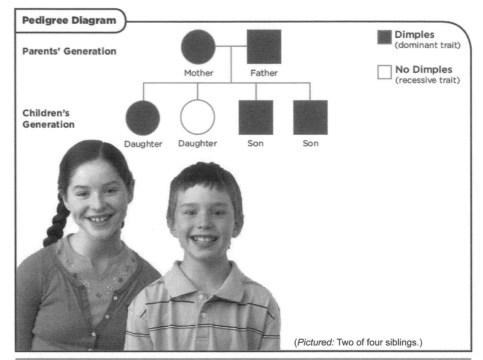

A tree diagram appears in the upper half of Figure 3.6. The figure also contains an illustration feature (the picture of the girl and boy) that is designed to help decode the diagram.

As you look at the tree diagram in Figure 3.6, ask yourself the following questions:

- How is the information organized?
- What is the relationship of the photograph to the shading in the squares and circles?
- Is there some feature of the diagram that can help clarify the information that is being conveyed?

The viewer needs to realize that several illustrative techniques are employed in Figure 3.6.

1. The diagram is a mix of artistic drawing and real-life photographs.

2. The diagram includes an element we have not discussed before, called a *key*. The interpretation of the illustration depends on recognizing the importance of the key (in the upper right-hand corner in Figure 3.6), which explains the shaded and nonshaded boxes and circles. Without the key, it would be difficult to derive any meaning from the boxes and circles. The shaded boxes and circle represent parents and offspring (children) with dimples and the open (unshaded) circle represents an offspring who does not have dimples. Without recognizing that aspect of the diagram, it would be difficult to derive any meaning from the shaded boxes and circles.

   Although not directly stated or indicated, it can be inferred from the labels that males are represented with squares and that females are represented with circles. Why might it be that that information is not included in the key? Does that information even matter when considering the purpose of this diagram? Sometimes synthetic diagrams can contain too much information, which only adds to their complexity and increases the difficulty students have in trying to interpret them.

3. The information presented is organized in a hierarchy from parents to children. As noted, males are represented with squares and females are represented with circles.

To interpret a tree diagram, the viewer needs to pay close attention to the various features incorporated in its design. Today, many computer program menus make use of the tree diagram structure to organize their features into categories that are easy to navigate.

Cyclical Diagrams

Cyclical diagrams are very common in science texts because they are well suited for describing continuous or renewable processes. These diagrams also can vary greatly in their complexity and can require considerable cognitive effort to interpret and analyze.

How does the diagram in Figure 3.7 differ from the one in Figure 3.5? Are different analytical skills required to interpret the two diagrams?

In Figure 3.7, the viewer gains information by reading the title. However, although the arrows indicate a single directional path, it is unclear where to begin (or end). Without a clear starting point, the diagram appears to be repetitive in its organization. When you ask students where to start when describing this diagram, you help emphasize that the cyclical technique represents a continuous series of events or stages where no one stage can be considered the starting point. The cyclical technique might remind students of the proverbial problem "Which came first—the chicken or the egg?" Also interesting to note in this particular diagram is that the individual representative size of the objects is not important when representing the concept of the pine tree life cycle. Hence the concern of relative size or scale is not critical for interpreting the illustration.

Figure 3.7 Pine Tree Life Cycle

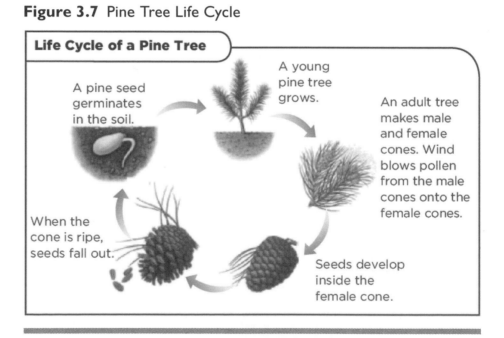

Source: Hackett, J. K., R. H. Moyer, and J. Vasquez. 2008. *Science A Closer Look*. Grade 5, Visual Literacy. Columbus, OH: Macmillan/McGraw-Hill, p. 18. Copyright © 2008 Macmillan/McGraw-Hill. Reprinted with permission.

Web Diagrams

Web diagrams show many interconnecting lines or arrows linking the parts of the subject in a network of relationships. Web diagrams are useful for showing the relationship among many aspects of an object, topic, or concept. However, the interconnecting lines can make the web diagram appear confusing or complex because they show multiple directions of processes rather than a single path. Study the web diagram in Figure 3.8. Then, think about how you decoded the information depicted in the diagram. For example, consider these questions:

- Did you begin by reading the title and then looking at all of the labeled images?
- Did you instead start by focusing on a single image and then trying to follow the arrows that lead away from it or to it?

Also ask yourself, Is there a single path moving through the entire diagram or are there multiple paths that do not always connect?

Adding to the complexity of this diagram is the cutaway view below the water and the lack of size comparisons among the representative organisms (that is, each organism is roughly the same size in the diagram even though in real life, the sizes of the organisms vary quite a bit). Does this lack of scale make it hard to interpret the diagram? Or does it help provide a clearer focus for the viewer? Another question to consider is whether the arrows in this diagram have the same meaning as they did in the linear diagram of the pond food web (Figure 3.5) or do they represent something different? How would you know?

Figure 3.8 A Pond Food Web

Source: Hackett, J. K., R. H. Moyer, and J. Vasquez. 2008. *Science A Closer Look.* Grade 3, Visual Literacy. Columbus, OH: Macmillan/McGraw-Hill, p.16. Copyright © 2008 Macmillan/McGraw-Hill. Reprinted with permission.

Sometimes the interconnecting lines in a web diagram—which show multiple directions of processes rather than a single path—can make the diagram confusing or overly complex for a student. One technique for helping students interpret these more complex web diagrams is to have them write words or phrases on the arrows, giving them a working text to describe the concepts or ideas being conveyed. For example, on the line from the pond grass to the pond snail a student might write "is eaten by." Or, on the line from the crayfish to the eastern painted turtle, the student might write "transfers energy to." By writing words or phrases on the lines, students build visual-verbal bridges; they link the big ideas portrayed in the diagram to simple verbal descriptions.

The arrows in the diagram in Figure 3.8 represent the flow of energy through the food web. In the linear diagram the source of that energy is clearly identified; in the web diagram that source is not indicated. Does the title "A Pond Food Web" provide enough meaning to the viewer to understand what the arrows represent? Do not assume that students recognize what information is being conveyed in a diagram. Rather, engage the class in an explicit discussion to emphasize the concept being presented.

The Flow of Information in Synthetic Diagrams

It is important to remind students that in the synthetic diagrams discussed in this chapter the process or information "flows" through the diagram. They can trace this flow with their fingers. Using their fingers helps students follow the flow of information—whether it is in a straight linear chain, in a more complex cyclical design that includes multiple pathways, or in a hierarchy such as a tree diagram.

As with analytic diagrams, students need to be cognitively alert when viewing synthetic diagrams in order to make sense of the information being conveyed. In addition to the questions they may have asked themselves with the analytic diagrams, they also need to consider these additional questions when analyzing synthetic diagrams:

- Does the diagram have a starting point or is there more than one point of entry?
- Does the diagram have captions, and if so, are they critical to interpreting the information in the diagram? Do they provide supporting details for easier analysis?

- Does the diagram show a series of steps in a process or is it an organized list of ideas?
- Is there a hierarchy to the information or does the diagram help provide a structure for organization?
- Does the diagram have a key—or other words or pictures—that provides information to help the viewer analyze the diagram?
- What do the arrows or lines connecting the images represent?

Although both tree diagrams and web diagrams can rely on picture elements, many times they are drawn without pictures. The complexity of the topic may warrant the use of words and arrows alone (without graphic images) to convey relationships. In such cases, tree diagrams and web diagrams resemble graphs and tables, depicting a large quantity of information in an organized or structured format.

Summary

The ease with which teachers today are able to generate and incorporate computer-based graphics into their teaching underscores the importance of teaching students how to make sense of what they see. The ability to read images is important because images can convey information that the spoken word cannot—information that people may not otherwise comprehend. Part of inquiry-based science instruction, which provides the foundation for scientific literacy, is the development of higher-order thinking skills. Visual literacy is an example of a higher-order thinking skill for analyzing and interpreting all forms of visual representations that depict the big ideas and themes of science.

Without specific instruction and modeling of the mental processes used for the interpretation of visuals, the acquisition of science concepts is far more difficult and challenging than it needs to be. The decoding of symbols is more than just learning how to read and write; it is an integral aspect of becoming a fully literate and productive citizen.

CHAPTER 3

CHAPTER 4
Creating Visual Thinking Tools

Have you ever tried to secure a screw into a piece of wood using a hammer? Or sew a button on a shirt using a pin? Or peel an apple using scissors?

Although you may have attempted such tasks because you were desperate (or inventive), you knew that you were simply using the wrong tool for the task. On its own, each tool is a wonderful thing. The hammer, pin, and scissors are each constructed in a particular way to accomplish the task for which they were specifically designed. The hammer's design is best suited for driving the pointed end of nails into wood. The head on the pin helps it to secure two pieces of fabric together without sliding out. The sharp edges of the scissors are better for cutting than for peeling (although one of the authors of this book does admit to using them in that manner on more than one occasion).

In today's educational landscape, teachers are faced with the challenge of differentiating their instructional approaches to accommodate the diverse backgrounds and experiences of the students in their classrooms. They must select the most appropriate "tools" in order to meet those individual needs. Being able to connect what students need to know with ways for them to use and recall this information has at times been problematic. Recent advances in brain research have shown that linking verbal or linguistic information with visual representations can improve a student's retention and increase their conceptual understanding. These visual representations can be called "visual thinking tools." How students select and create these tools and then apply them to their learning experiences can facilitate their acquisition of information. In this chapter we will look at a variety of visual thinking tools, describe how these visuals can support your science instruction, and discuss strategies for helping students recognize that advantage.

Please read the following passage. As you read, think about how you are mentally organizing the information in order to make sense of it. Then read the passage a second time and think about how you would share this information with someone who has not read the passage.

Sedimentary rock—
Dolostone

The Rock Cycle

There are three types of rocks: igneous, sedimentary, and metamorphic.

The elements that make up rocks are never created or destroyed, although they can be redistributed, transforming one rock type to another. The core, mantle, and crust of the Earth can be envisioned as a giant rock-recycling machine. The recycling machine works something like this. Molten (liquid) rock material solidifies either at or below the surface of the Earth to form igneous rocks. Uplifting occurs, forming mountains made of rock. The exposure of rocks to weathering and erosion at the Earth's surface breaks them down into smaller grains, producing soil. The grains (soil) are transported by wind, water, and gravity and eventually deposited as sediments. This process is referred to as erosion. The sediments are deposited in layers and become compacted and cemented (lithified), forming sedimentary rocks.

Variation in temperature, pressure, and/or the chemistry of the rock can cause chemical and/or physical changes in igneous and sedimentary rocks to form metamorphic rocks. When exposed to higher temperatures, metamorphic rocks (or any other rock type for that matter) may be partially melted, resulting in the creation once again of igneous rocks—starting the cycle all over again.*

Igneous rock—
Olivine basalt

Metamorphic rock—*Quartzite*

*This passage can be found at *www. rocksandminerals. com.* It is also an NSTA scilink: *www. rocksandminerals.com/rockcycle.htm,* recommended for use in grades 5–8.

What was this passage about? As you were reading, what were you thinking? Were you thinking, "Rocks! Ugh! I don't understand this stuff." Or were you (we hope!) trying to picture how the information on the three types of rocks fits together? When you read the phrase, "There are three types of rocks," did you perhaps have a mental image of a three-column chart (Figure 4.1) for the three types of rocks?

Figure 4.1 Column Heads for Chart of Three Kinds of Rocks

Igneous	Sedimentary	Metamorphic

As you read further,

- did that mental image change because of the addition of more information, such as the phrase "rock-recycling machine?"
- did the word *recycle* indicate to you an ongoing process? If so, how did that change your initial mental image of a chart with three columns (if such an image was what you started with)?
- did you, in your mind, "see" the three types of rocks in a different arrangement, such as the flow diagram in Figure 4.2?
- did your mental image change even further as more information was added?
- how did you begin to fill in the new details about the rock types in your mind?
- how does the image in Figure 4.3 (p. 42) help organize or clarify the particular details found in the passage?
- did you consider adding arrow heads to the lines connecting the different types of rocks in order to signify motion or process?

Figure 4.2 Flow Diagram for Three Kinds of Rocks

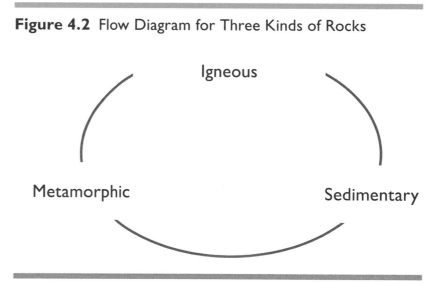

As you reread the passage, did you add even more details and words to your mental image to make the meaning even clearer or more explicit? Did you pause to think about vocabulary words you were unfamiliar with in order to remember them? Does the placement of the words on the arrows in Figure 4.3 help clarify what action or process is occurring between each type of rock? Look at the image in Figure 4.4 for an even more elaborate diagram on the three kinds of rocks.

Figure 4.3 Flow Diagram for Simple Relationship Among Three Kinds of Rocks

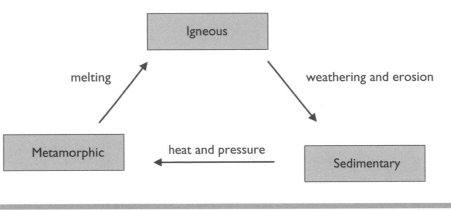

Figure 4.4 Flow Diagram for Complex Relationships Among Three Kinds of Rocks

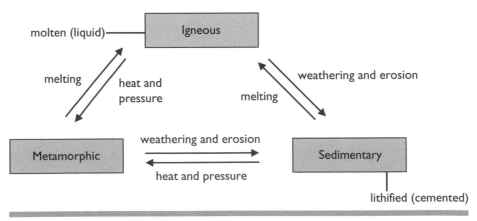

CHAPTER 4

Types of Visual Thinking Tools

By developing visual thinking tools, such as charts and diagrams, students acquire formats for recalling, retelling, or making meaning from written text. As adults, we tend to create such mental pictures intuitively as we read information. Creating these mental pictures helps us organize facts and details as we seek to find an organization or pattern to the words and their meanings. Many students who struggle in school do so because they fail to detect the patterns that link their everyday learning experiences together. Caine and Caine (1994) have described the brain as a "pattern detector." People who fail to recognize patterns are bound to struggle to organize the massive amounts of sensory input bombarding their brains each day—and so they are often unable to link the input to something meaningful or significant.

Visual thinking tools help us create the patterns that our brains need to facilitate our learning and thinking. The three main types of visual thinking tools are brainstorm webs, graphic organizers, and concept maps. Each of these tools helps transform words, thoughts, and ideas into visual representations for organizing, translating, and transmitting our thinking. These tools can vary from simple line drawings sketched on scrap paper to highly organized and structured diagrams.

Figure 4.5 Brainstorm Web

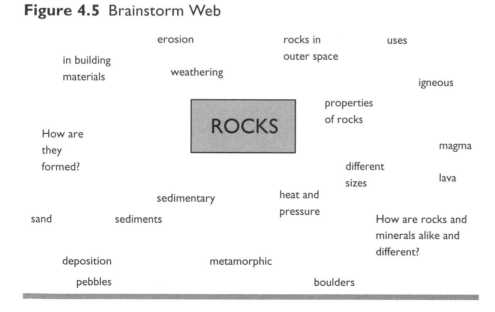

Brainstorm Webs

Brainstorm webs are ways to generate and categorize a multitude of ideas and thoughts. They can be used to list attributes, definitions, or facts that are usually related to a single concept or theme. As their name implies, they can be most useful when generating fresh ideas quickly and are especially useful in the creative/development phase of a project where many ideas can be generated without evaluation or critique. Although they do present a model of organizing the information, their physical appearance tends to be unstructured and randomly constructed. This "chaotic" array can be confusing to students at first. The example in Figure 4.5 (p. 43) depicts the random nature of the brainstorm web.

Simple Graphic Organizers

Graphic organizers are visual tools that allow the viewer to detect patterns in information and organize them to facilitate the viewer's understanding. (In Chapter 5 we look at the three-dimensional graphic organizer, a more complex organizer than discussed here.) Graphic organizers are a common tool among teachers and are used across disciplines because of the graphic organizers' simplicity and commonality in function. Figure 4.6 shows a graphic organizer used to present the main idea (sedimentary rock) and its corresponding supporting details.

Figure 4.6 Main Idea and Supporting Details Graphic Organizer

Main Idea	Details
Sedimentary rock forms in layers from deposited materials	Results from erosion of other types of rocks
	Examples include sandstone, limestone, and conglomerate
	Uses include construction, energy, art

It should be noted that although these visual tools can help students see the relationships among parts of a whole or make comparisons between groups of objects, they tend to be limited to specific content tasks associated with skills—for example, comparing and contrasting or identifying main idea and details. Sometimes, these visual tools are precomposed frames in which the student just fills in missing information; using visual tools in this way reduces students' interest and motivation. The frames may provide the structure lacking in brainstorming webs but at the same time they limit the creativity of the user. For these reasons, they should be used sparingly.

Concept Maps

Concept maps communicate complex interrelated ideas and relationships built around a single concept, but they can be overwhelming to students when it comes to describing or making use of the information they contain. A concept map is a special type of synthetic web diagram in which the cells (or nodes) identify main ideas flowing from a central theme or concept; lines are used to link supporting information together. These links can be labeled and include arrowheads that can provide directionality to the viewer, but the lines sometimes add to the complexity of the visual. In Figure 4.7, the concept map provides better organizations than the brainstorm web but can appear random and confusing to the casual observer.

Figure 4.7 Concept Map

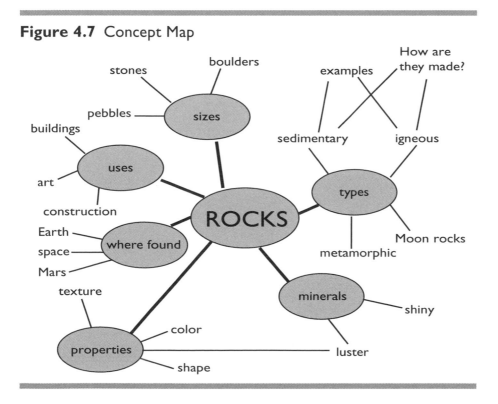

CHAPTER 4

Visual Thinking Tools and the Brain

As researchers continue to learn about the brain and how it works, our use and creation of visuals in the classroom becomes ever more important. Recent research (see, for example, pp. 5–7) indicates that the brain, mostly through its visual receptors, is constantly processing incoming bits of information—trying to make sense of it, to assess its importance, and to assign some relevance to it. This processing involves the complex interactions of emotion, attention, and relevance. The role of emotion in student learning can best be summed up by a quote from the PBS series *The Secret Life of the Brain:* "The brain is not a thinking machine, but a feeling machine that thinks" (Hyerle 2004, p. 26). This quotation underscores how emotions can influence the processing of information. Information processing is obstructed by stressful conditions as the body's natural response mechanisms work on the fight-or-flight reaction: Do I prepare for battle or do I prepare to flee? Neurotransmitters in the brain activate the limbic system, which is responsible for action, and not the cortex region, which is responsible for planning, rational thought, and decision making. The fight-or-flight response is useful for survival, but not for learning.

As information pours in through our senses, the brain works to make meaning of it. The brain tries to organize, evaluate, and analyze the importance of the information. Once the brain determines that the input is necessary and has some emotional importance attached to it, the conscious process of information storage begins. The short-term (working) memory "chunks" these incoming bits of information together to keep the working memory from becoming overloaded by the constant stream of data. The construction of visual tools helps the brain actively string this incoming information together by forming patterns. These patterns help mark neural pathways that are needed for long-term retention. Gerlic and Jausovec (1999), who investigated the cognitive processes in learning information, observed that explicit engagement of students in the creation of nonlinguistic representations stimulated and increased activity in their brains. Thus we can conclude that students who create their own visual thinking tools are building the mental capabilities of pattern recognition essential for helping them make meaning of—and retain—the information they are learning.

Applications for Teachers and Students

Look back at the introductory passages in "The Rock Cycle" (p. 40). Which of the graphic organizers below (Figure 4. 8 or Figure 4. 9) would be best for developing the skill of identifying the main idea and supporting details based on the information in the passage? Complete the graphic organizer that you think is best for organizing the information. (You will probably find that the organizer you choose does not provide enough space to completely "recompose" the information you read. Just go as far as you can with the given boxes or ovals.)

Figure 4.8 Graphic Organizer–Chart

Main Idea	Details

Figure 4.9 Graphic Organizer–Bubble

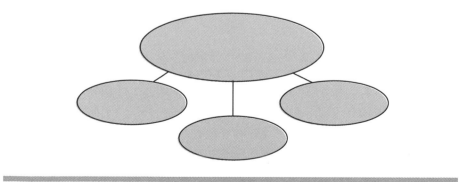

CHAPTER 4

Students can develop their reading skills by using the structures in these graphic organizers to indicate the relationship between the main idea and the details in a paragraph or longer piece of writing. Younger students in particular will need explicit instruction to understand the purpose of the organizers.

Once students understand how to use a graphic organizer to organize information, teachers should encourage them to create whichever structure—that is, the chart or the bubble—works best for them. Graphic organizers help students by providing structure for organizing new information; at the same time, however, using premade charts can restrict students' creativity and active engagement in a task. Simply putting information into the organizer does not make students active participants in the meaning-making phase of learning nor does it encourage them to feel that the task is important or relevant. The emphasis should be on *creating* the chart or bubble, not on its completion. A teacher who is in the habit of using premade frames for students to complete reduces the emotional connections and the sense of relevance necessary for a student's brain to move knowledge into long-term memory, where learning occurs. Marcia Tate put it best in the title of her book: *Worksheets Don't Grow Dendrites* (Tate 2010).

Now create your own graphic organizer. On a blank sheet of paper, visually organize the information from the passage on the rock cycle (p. 40). Afterward, think about how this visual tool helped you describe the processes involved in the rock cycle. Think about the words you used to describe your thinking as you were creating this visual map. How did these words reflect what you know?

Summary

Brainstorm webs, graphic organizers, and concept maps have been important tools for classroom teachers for the past 30 years. Teachers find that these visual tools promote classroom discussions and conversations in which students use words that reveal their thinking processes—always helpful information for teachers, particularly for formative assessment. From the students' point of view, the tools provide a frame of reference for them

48

to reflect on what they already know. This metacognitive step of reflection allows the student to regulate the processing of the vast number of bits of information being taken in and to make the necessary connections among facts, feelings, and the purposes for knowing. Such reflection helps students become positive and confident about their knowledge and learning.

CHAPTER 4

CHAPTER 5
Three-Dimensional Graphic Organizers ("Foldables")

Have you ever sat in a meeting where someone was doodling? It might even have been you. Our brains are continuously scanning the constant bombardment of information they are receiving in order to make sense of it. We try to fit new information into our existing knowledge networks where the information might be stored. Doodling is actually a way that some people process new information. The doodles may be in the form of concept maps, abstract pictures, curly lines, or organized lists. The brain is determined to try and distinguish between what is meaningful information and what is not. If the information is neither meaningful nor tied to anything the brain considers useful, then more than likely the "forgetting curve" will go into effect and the information will be discarded.

If teachers want learners to retain and understand new information, the best way to help students' brains manage this input is by organizing the information in some useable, recallable way. Three-dimensional graphic organizers, sometimes called *foldables* (Zike 2000, 2006, 2008), are effective student-created tools that can help this management process occur. (See "Teaching the Way You Want to Be Taught," p. 53, for a first-person account by Dinah Zike of how she came to develop foldables first for her own use, then for her students' use.) Three-dimensional graphic organizers are analogous to information on an index card. Students choose from a variety of ways to fold colored paper and create a model with pictures and text that best represents the information they are trying to learn. As one third-grade student said, "Foldables help me see the information in my head and this gives me a way to organize it."

Three-dimensional graphic organizers allow learners to record and process new words and concepts in a hands-on, kinesthetic way. Without even being conscious of it, they will be attaching relevance, meaning, and emotion to their three-dimensional "products." This visual literacy tool also helps increase students' visual-spatial thinking, which research has shown to be critical to long-term understanding. As defined by the National Research Council, spatial thinking is

> a constructive amalgam of three elements: concept of space, tools of representation, and processes of reasoning. Space provides the conceptual and analytical framework within which data can be integrated, related, and structured into a whole. Representations—either internal and cognitive or external and graphic, linguistic, physical, and so forth—provide the forms within which structured information can be stored, analyzed, comprehended, and communicated to others. Reasoning processes provide the means of manipulating, interpreting, and explaining the structured information. (NRC 2006, p. 25)

As we begin to explore the three-dimensional graphic organizer, please keep in mind that it is only one technique for improving students' visual literacy skills and for helping students retain new learning. It is not meant to replace any other effective means that students use to collect, record, and organize data, especially science logs or science journals. However, the three-dimensional graphic organizer *can* greatly enhance the usefulness and purpose of the *science notebook*, which combines the data collection portions of a laboratory log book with the self-reflection and analysis aspects of a journal (Klentschy 2008, 2010). In the creation of their science notebooks, students not only record data and information; they also continue to develop the metacognitive skill of reflection. By adding the three-dimensional graphic organizers

Teaching the Way You Want to Be Taught

Imagine attending a session at a science conference, eagerly anticipating what you might learn. The featured speaker establishes his or her credentials, distributes a handout, and asks participants to read the handout and answer questions in writing. You are informed that the session lasts 50 minutes and there will be a short discussion at the end. How many of you would walk out of that session to find one that was more interesting and challenging and that presented information in multiple formats? I would!

As teachers, we expect presentations by experts who use a variety of methods that target our different learning styles and learning preferences. My learning preference is to be visually, kinesthetically, and aurally stimulated by someone presenting valuable information based on his or her experiences—not by reading and working on a handout in a 50-minute session.

Though I might walk out of a presentation, students can't walk out of a science classroom. If a science teacher favors an auditory style of teaching, the students in his or her class who are visual and/or kinesthetic learners will have to work extra hard to adapt to the teacher's auditory style—and in some cases the students won't even try to adapt. I liken this scenario to being a left-handed person in a right-handed world. It can be managed, but it takes work and adaptation, and some students might not make the extra effort on their own (or even realize that it is called for). How much more learning could take place if all learning styles were addressed at all times? Imagine what might happen if all of a student's energy could be focused on the process of learning instead of adapting!

As a visual/kinesthetic learner attending a school with a predominantly auditory teaching style in the 1960s, I seemed to face the reverse scenario: I was a right-handed person forced to use my left hand to survive. I adapted by folding and cutting paper into sections that corresponded to the number of main ideas I had jotted down in notes during a lecture or while reading a text. I recorded supporting facts, terms definitions, questions I needed answered, and other information under tabs. As an after-school tutor, I used my folded-and-cut paper study aids to help other students visually organize information. My personal need to adapt auditory teaching to my visual/kinesthetic learning style eventually resulted in the three-dimensional graphic organizers called foldables. I am proud that over the past 40 years my foldables have become one of many visual literacy tools for teachers and students alike.

As a reader of this book, you have no doubt already discovered that *Developing Visual Literacy in Science, K–8* offers a multitude of proven visual literacy tools, including foldables, for use in the classroom. I'm sure you will find strategies here that you can use to teach the way you want to be taught!

Dinah Zike
Dinah-Might Adventures, LP
www.dinah.com

to their notebooks, students use organizational skills that help them recall factual information and that provide a format for explanation and interpretation of their scientific evidence. The graphic organizer can also be used as a study tool and as an assessment device.

Three-dimensional graphic organizers can be used in different content areas and for different purposes. In this chapter we show six kinds of organizers: four-shutter, three-section accordion, layered, Venn diagram, top-tab, and two-shutter. We give a grade-level range from which each example was taken to provide some context for the example; however, all of these foldables can be done with students at every grade level. In the primary grades, younger students may need a bit more help with the cutting and folding, but once they are familiar with the construction of foldables there is no stopping what they can manage. This is by no means a complete list of kinds of three-dimensional graphic organizers, nor are we showing the complete lessons for which these organizers might be used. The examples are meant to give you an idea of how the organizers can be used within a science lesson. For a list of the many ways to use this tool, Google "three-dimensional organizers" or visit Dinah-Might Adventures at *www.dinah.com* for more information.

Grades K–4, Using Foldables in Life Science

When teaching about cycles or ongoing processes, teachers often find the four-shutter foldable to be useful. It provides for the separation of distinct phases within a four-stage cycle, such as the frog life cycle (Figures 5.1a and 5.1b).

Grades 5–8, Using Foldables in Life Science

Imagine that a class of fifth and sixth graders is learning about living and nonliving organisms and how they interact in an ecosystem. They begin this lesson with an inquiry activity: They mark off an area on the school grounds and collect data on all the living and nonliving things inside that area. After a class discussion about their recorded observations in their data charts, they are ready to delve into some informational text reading. The students read and discuss the following information:

Figure 5.1a Frog Life Cycle
(Four-Shutter Foldable, closed)

Figure 5.1b Frog Life Cycle: Tadpole
(Four-Shutter Foldable, open)

Biotic and Abiotic Factors

Who or what is around you right now? You probably see classmates or your teacher. Perhaps there are books. You might be sitting at your desk while reading. There are both living and nonliving things in your environment. Scientists call the living things in an environment *biotic factors*. Plants, animals, and bacteria are all biotic factors. You are a biotic factor too!

Your desk, pen, pencil, and textbook are *abiotic factors*. Abiotic factors are the nonliving things in an environment. Other abiotic factors are water, rocks, soil, and light. Climate is another abiotic factor; the word *climate* refers to the typical weather of an environment.

The biotic and abiotic factors of an environment make up an *ecosystem*. An ecosystem can be small, like a single log, or very large, like a desert. All living things in an ecosystem depend on the nonliving things to survive. For example, to breathe and lay eggs, a frog depends on the air and the water in a pond. The living things also depend on one another.

Each organism in an ecosystem has its own place to live, called a *habitat*. Different ecosystems provide very different habitats. A penguin could not find a habitat to meet its needs in a hot, dry desert. Likewise a cactus would not be able to survive in a pond ecosystem.

The foldables pictured on pages 55, 57, 58, 59, and 60 were constructed for use in this book by Frankie Troutman, a veteran elementary school teacher and one of the authors of the book. These visual literacy tools are normally constructed in the classroom by students.

This is a lot of information for students to try to understand. In addition, the passage uses four terms that are likely to be new to the students: *biotic factor, abiotic factor, ecosystem,* and *habitat.* The teacher now introduces the students to a technique called recomposing to make their three-dimensional organizers. Recomposing is a way for them to collect new information and develop an understanding of the vocabulary terms. Michaels, Shouse, and Schweingruber (2008) note that "modeling involves the construction and testing of representations that are analogous to systems in the real world. These representations can take many forms, including physical models, computer programs, diagrams, and mathematical equations and propositions" (p. 109). When students recompose, they take information from one form (e.g., from a reading selection, from data collected in an experiment, by listening to someone talk, or by watching a video) and summarize or record it in another, visual form, such as in a diagram, table, graphic organizer, or drawing. In recomposing, students must synthesize information, identifying its most salient points. They cannot simply copy their sources; rather, they need to think about the highlights of information they are learning, design how they are going to summarize those highlights as a visual, and then work to accomplish that task (Michaels, Shouse, and Schweingruber 2008).

Real-life scientists frequently share formulas, theories, laboratory techniques, and scientific information by calling on effective verbal means to communicate and disseminate their findings. They also share their ideas and observations in a myriad of visual ways, including written text, drawings, diagrams, formulas, and photographs. Students must likewise collaborate and communicate using spoken, written, and visual representations of the world. The students we have been discussing have been reading and learning what makes up an ecosystem. Now it is time for them to recompose this information into three-dimensional organizers that communicate their understanding and identify what information about that science concept they see as important. Students work alone or in groups as they build their information bases; however, each student eventually creates his or her own three-dimensional graphic organizer.

Figure 5.2a Pond Ecosystem (Three-Section Accordion Foldable, closed)

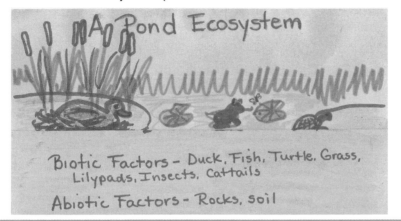

Figure 5.2b Pond Ecosystem (Three-Section Accordion Foldable, open)

Let's say that the students decided to show a pond ecosystem using a three-section accordion fold. In Figure 5.2a (p. 57), the picture shows the closed "accordion" on which the students illustrated their pond ecosystem and listed the biotic and abiotic factors found in and around this ecosystem. In Figure 5.2b, the "accordion" is now open, showing a cutaway view of the inside of the pond with the biotic and abiotic elements.

With three-dimensional graphic organizers, students take large amounts of information they need to process and organize it into manageable segments. They scaffold their thinking and organize it for better retention and recall. As the students in our example continue their study of ecosystems, the teacher introduces the concept of biomes. The teacher identifies a biome as a large ecosystem that has its own kinds of plants, animals, and soil as well as patterns of temperature and rainfall. (We are assuming here that the students have already had initial exposure through an activity to the vocabulary before they get to the content development section of the lesson.) After the teacher introduces the students to the six major biomes of the world—taiga, grassland, tropical rain forest, tundra, deciduous forest, and desert—the teacher instructs them to make layered foldables for recording their information. They are to list each biome on a tab, and under each tab they are to write about the biome's characteristics and where this type of biome could be found (see Figures 5.3a and 5.3b).

Figure 5.3a Biomes
(Layered Foldable, closed)

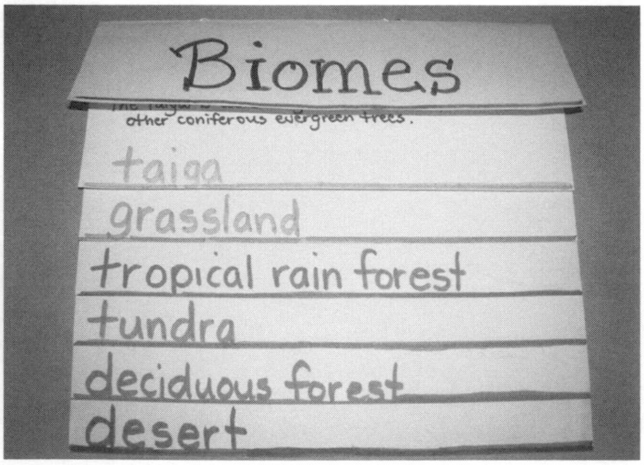

Figure 5.3b Biomes: Conditions of a Taiga (Layered Foldable, open)

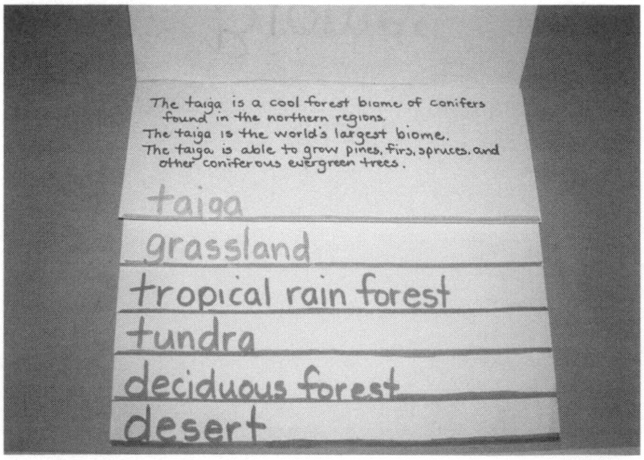

Another use of tabs in an organizer is shown in Figures 5.4a and 5.4b, where students are comparing and contrasting land animals with aquatic animals in a three-tab Venn diagram. Perhaps students in one class are organizing a list of the different classifications and characteristics of vertebrates. (See the National Science Education Standard under "Structure and Function in Living Things": "Living systems at all levels of organization demonstrate the complementary nature of structure and function" [NRC 1996, p. 156].) Students might construct a top-tab foldable as shown in figures 5.5a and 5.5b. This type of organizer can help them organize information *while* they are learning about each kind of vertebrate. It provides a way to categorize information by separating the individual subgroups from the larger main group.

Eventually, you can put together all of the graphic organizers the students have created into a student portfolio by making a two-shutter foldable as shown in figures 5.6a and 5.6b (p. 60). Or you could always have the students place their graphic organizers directly into their

Figure 5.4a Land and Aquatic Animals (Venn Diagram Foldable, closed)

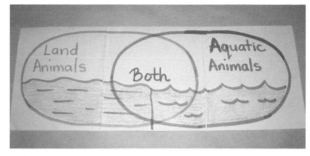

Figure 5.4b Shared Characteristic of Amphibians (Venn Diagram Foldable, open)

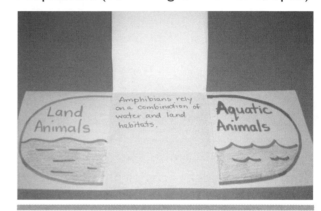

Figure 5.5a Vertebrates (Top-Tab Foldable, closed)

Figure 5.5b Vertebrates—Amphibians (Top-Tab Foldable, open)

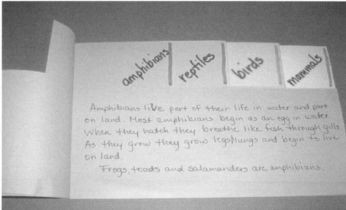

Figure 5.6a Animal Life
Student Portfolio
(Two-Shutter Foldable, closed)

Figure 5.6b Animal Life Student Portfolio
(Two-Shutter Foldable, open)

Figure 5.7 Student Science Notebook With
Foldables Pasted In

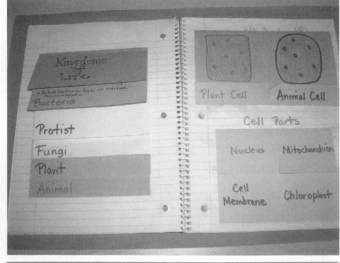

student notebooks as shown in Figure 5.7. As students build their experiences with three-dimensional graphic organizers, they will learn to make meaning from the text they are reading or from the information they are hearing. These organizers can be thought of as summary notes or visual reminders of the new information they have acquired. The more tools we can give students to help with their meaning-making abilities, the more powerful the learning experiences will be for them.

A Note on Vocabulary Building: As science teachers, we know that the body of science content knowledge that students must learn as they progress through the grade levels is very large. We also realize that there is what seems like an overwhelming number of new vocabulary words, or "academic language," contained in this body of knowledge that students must internalize. New vocabulary terms in science have traditionally been taught in simple recall fashion. We now know that by using hands-on activities and discussion our students can begin to actually comprehend the meaning of these words, not just memorize their definitions. Using three-dimensional organizers as a tool for connecting text to pictures provides for effective vocabulary instruction and the vocabulary can be more easily integrated into different contexts, including subjects outside the science classroom.

Summary

Science educators and researchers agree that the most important goal for science learning today should be firing up learners' brain circuitry by actively engaging them in their own learning processes. Increasingly, science teachers are adopting the inquiry approach, which leads to fundamental changes in their relationships with their students. The teacher becomes a facilitator or guide for the student's own process of exploration, discovery, and understanding. Real learning is no longer considered to consist of accumulating a specific body of knowledge or the memorization of correct answers; rather, we now know that real learning is the process of exploration and discovery, processes that are driven by curiosity. We can foster this new approach to teaching science content by providing visual literacy tools to students to (1) help them connect to the new information they are learning and (2) make this new information both coherent and applicable to their current understanding.

Whenever a teacher asks us why he or she should take the time to use three-dimensional graphic organizers, we say it is because the organizers

- provide a system for organizing, displaying, and arranging data—making it easier for students to grasp science concepts, theories, processes, facts, and ideas;
- offer a multitude of creative formats in which students can present projects, research, experimental results, and inquiry-based reports;

- incorporate the use of fundamental skills such as comparing and contrasting, recognizing cause and effect, and finding similarities and differences; and
- give the teacher an alternative assessment tool with which to evaluate students' progress and give students ways to evaluate their own progress.

CHAPTER 6
Visual Literacy in Life Science:
Insect Metamorphosis

"Visual tools are a breakthrough in education and
not just another tool on the sagging tool belt of
endless and uncoordinated 'best practices'
for teachers."

—David Hyerle 2009, p. 2

We invite you to come with us on a learning journey.
Chapters 6, 7, and 8 are designed to help you practice your visual literacy teaching strategies. Even though each of these chapters follows the same format, each one addresses a different content area: life science (insect metamorphosis), Earth science (phases of the Moon), and physical science (force and motion). We hope you find these activities helpful and that you will use them not only in your classroom but in your professional learning groups as well (see sidebar on p. 65).

Third-grade teacher Stacey Greene, who worked with us on Chapters 6–8, has written the introduction to your learning journey on page 64. Stacey teaches at Hopi Elementary School in Scottsdale, Arizona. She is a recipient of a Presidential Award for Excellence in Mathematics and Science (2006) and has earned her National Board Certification (2008).

Dear Teachers,

I have taught science in elementary school for many years. It is my passion, and I have even won recognition for my teaching. When I first read the visual literacy research, I thought, *That makes perfect sense. But will it transfer to my class? Will it make a difference for my kids?*

Having followed the guidance in Chapters 6, 7, and 8, I can say unequivocally, *It does!* The gains I saw in my students after just one of the lessons was phenomenal. When I applied these lessons in my science classes, my students came up with better questions, noticed more, made inferences, and retained more of the lesson information than ever before. The base I built with these lessons has carried over into our science instruction on a regular basis.

In addition, my students have applied the techniques they learned in science to their social studies lessons, especially when reading informational text. As a teacher who is always struggling against the minutes allotted for a subject, I found this integration of skills to be a huge bonus.

We all teach students who understand in many ways, at many different levels, and at many speeds. When you consider that some of these students don't even speak our language, the challenge is clear! Instruction in visual understanding—being able to decode and use information through visuals—has been a powerful way to meet that challenge. Chapters 6, 7, and 8 give you lessons to apply directly into your classroom. I hope you, like me, will see immediate results.

Enjoy the learning journey,

Stacey Greene

Teachers need and want dynamic breakthroughs that will help improve their craft. In Chapters 6, 7, and 8, we show you ways to apply the visual literacy tools you have been reading about in this book. Please keep in mind that the inquiry-based activities in each chapter are not full science lessons but portions of the 5E Instructional Model (Bybee et al. 2006). This model moves students through predictable and consistent stages of learning: Engage, Explore, Explain, Elaborate, and Evaluate. In the following chapters, we provide examples of the Engage and Explore stages of the learning model in order to provide a context for the Explain stage, which is the stage in which the use of visuals most often occurs. We offer a suggested sequence of how a science lesson can unfold and we identify places in your lesson where various visual literacy tools can be used most effectively.

Using *Developing Visual Literacy in Science, K–8* for Professional Development

Large Groups

(Requires a minimum of six two-hour sessions)

Session 1:   Prior to the first session, assign Chapter 1. Spend the first session developing an agreed-upon operational definition of *visual literacy* and discuss Chapter 1. For the next meeting, assign each of Chapters 2–5 to different groups.

Sessions 2–4:   Each group teaches the larger group about the chapter it has been assigned. (All participants will be responsible for the learning in all the chapters.) Allow time for group processing. Teachers can begin to try some of the visual literacy strategies in their own classrooms. Assign the practice chapters (6–8) for the next session.

Session 5:   Use this session for group discussion of Chapters 6–8 and for checking for understanding. Ask each participant to take one of his or her own existing science lessons and develop visual literacy strategies for that lesson. This could be done in grade-level teams or individually.

Session 6:   Discuss the lessons with the visual literacy strategies inserted.

Professional Learning Communities (PLCs)

1. Read the introduction independently and discuss at the first meeting.

2. Read Chapters 1–5 independently and discuss. After the discussion of each chapter and before the next PLC, try the visual literacy strategy that has been discussed in that chapter and be ready to share at the next meeting.

3. From Chapters 6–8, choose the content area that is closest to the science topic you are working on at the present time and form groups based on the three content areas. Discuss the chapter in groups. Each participant then takes a lesson from his or her own curriculum and decides where to insert and practice the visual literacy skills and strategies from Chapter 6, 7, or 8. Try this updated version of the lesson in your classroom.

4. In the next PLC, compare results, comments, and discoveries about the lesson.

5. Divide into teams of teachers and collaborate on a unit of study.

Districtwide Inservice (by Grade Level)

1. Assuming the inservice is for one day only, use the morning of the inservice day to go through theory and one lesson example.

2. In the afternoon, grade-level teams, using their district curricula, provide examples of visual literacy strategies that will help students effectively learn the science content.

3. Post suggestions for using the strategies in grade-level science lessons on the district website (i.e., create a "lesson bank"). With a districtwide lesson bank, teachers share resources, pictures, and units.

As Dutch post-impressionist painter Vincent Van Gogh (1853–1890) said, "A good picture is equivalent to a good deed." We hope that the partial lessons in Chapters 6, 7, and 8 will be the "good deeds" to get you on the path to incorporating visual literacy strategies into your lessons.

"All About Praying Mantises"

Teacher Background for Grades K–4 and 5–8

The praying mantis is a carnivorous insect. But it is not a pest! It is actually an organic form of pest control because it eats lots of unwanted insects and, unfortunately, some wanted ones as well. There are about 2,000 different species worldwide, which range in size from about 1 cm to more than 30 cm long. There are approximately 20 species that are native to the United States. They range in color from a pea green to brown and even a shade of pink. The name *praying mantis* comes from the fact that the folding of their front legs looks like a posture of prayer.

Source: Maceribeyza, Creative Commons License

The praying mantis has a triangle-shaped head with a compound eye on each side. It is the only insect that can turn its head a full 180 degrees (some species can even turn their heads almost 300 degrees) without moving the rest of its body. A praying mantis can spot its prey (which include insects and other invertebrates such as beetles, butterflies, spiders, crickets, and grasshoppers) up to 18 m away and tends to ambush them very quickly. Its forelegs are spiked, which helps the mantis hold onto its victim, and its powerful jaws make it easy to kill its prey. With only one ear, which is found on its abdomen, a praying mantis can hear very high-pitched sounds. This ability mainly helps it escape other predators, such as bats.

Like all insects, praying mantises have six legs, but their front legs are not used for walking. All the legs are attached to the thorax. The mantis has four wings that are also attached to the thorax and that fold over the abdomen. In some species this gives the praying mantis the appearance of a leaf. The abdomen is segmented and contains the mantis's digestive and reproductive organs. Females have six abdominal segments and males have eight. An interesting fact is that when the mantis is mating the female bites off the head of the male. One theory for this unusual behavior is that this provides a needed source of protein for the female.

The young of many insects do not look anything like the adults. They go through a change in their body forms as they mature. This change in body form is called *metamorphosis*. There are two kinds of insect metamorphosis, *complete* and *incomplete*. Bees are an example of an insect that goes through *complete metamorphosis* as they go from egg, to larva, to pupa, and then to adult. Praying mantises go through *incomplete metamorphosis*, which has only three stages: from egg, to nymph (which looks like the adult only much smaller), and finally to adult. The nymph does go through several molts of the exoskeleton as it grows into an adult.

Praying mantises are mostly *diurnal* (active during the daytime), and many students may have seen or even held these harmless insects. There are many sites on the internet that sell mantis eggs, which can make for a fun science lesson. The mantises will live up to 12 months in captivity or they can be released when they reach adulthood.

Grades K–4, The Characteristics of Organisms

Objectives (K–4)

The student will be able to describe and compare how different insect parts help insects meet their needs.

Purpose (K–4)

This activity will help students observe that different insects have different body parts that help them meet their needs.

Materials (K–4)

- One hand lens for every two students
- Variety of plastic insects (each student group will receive three to six different insects)
- A science log for each student to record observations

Engage (K–4)

Begin by asking the following questions:

- What can you tell me about an insect that you have seen? (Allow students time to express their experiences and tell a bit about what types of insects they might have seen.)
- How does an ant move? How does a bee move? What about a grasshopper? (Ants walk and climb; bees walk and fly; grasshoppers can walk, hop, and fly.)

Share the following information with your students:

Each of the insects in your group has different body parts that help them walk, hop, and fly. We are going to take a closer look at many different kinds of insects. These insects are not alive. They are made of plastic. As we look closely at our insects, we are going to discuss with our group the parts we observe.

Explore (K–4)

Guiding Question: How do insects use their different body parts to help them meet their needs?

1. Divide the students into groups and pass out three to six different plastic insects to each group along with a hand lens.

2. Have the students observe their insects while you walk around to each group and help them focus on the main body parts (i.e., legs, eyes, mouth, wings [if they have them], body segments, and antennae). *Ask:*

MEETING THE STANDARD

K–4 *The Characteristics of Organisms:* Each plant or animal has different structures that serve different functions in growth, survival and reproduction. (p. 129)

National Science Education Standards (NRC 1996), Content Standard C: Life Science

CHAPTER 6

- Which parts do you think help the insects eat?
- Which body part helps an insect move around?
- Do your insects have eyes?
- What body parts are a mystery to you—that is, what are the parts of the insects that you don't know the reason for?
- How are the body parts of the different insects alike?
- Are there body parts on one insect you can't find on another?

3. *Ask:* How can you sort your insects into different groups (e.g., by color, body shape, overall size, wings/no wings, size of legs)?

4. After the student groups have had ample time to observe and discuss the different insect body parts, have them share their findings with the class. *Ask:* Have you seen any of these insects in the environment (around your yard or home)? If so, what did you see and what was the insect doing?

5. After the classroom discussion, have the students pick one or two of the insects to draw in their science notebooks, labeling as many of the body parts as they can. Depending on the students' grade levels, have them write one to three sentences about the function of each body part. (This step could also be completed after students have learned more about the body parts in the content development phase of the lesson.)

Grades 5–8, Reproduction and Heredity

Objectives (5–8)

The student will be able to describe and compare the stages of incomplete metamorphosis.

Purpose (5–8)

This activity will allow students to observe incomplete metamorphosis.

Materials (5–8)

This ongoing activity requires planning ahead! It will take at least four weeks and should be extended throughout the content development phase of the lesson. The students will make their observations as they compare and contrast the different stages of

MEETING THE STANDARD

5–8 *Reproduction and Heredity*: Reproduction is a characteristic of all living systems; because no individual organism lives forever, reproduction is essential to the continuation of every species. (p. 157)

National Science Education Standards (NRC 1996), Content Standard C: Life Science

CHAPTER 6

the insect's development. To make this a worthwhile experience, students need to actually observe praying mantis life stages. You will begin with praying mantis egg cases, which are easily accessible through many websites and science supply houses.* If you want to use a second insect so students can compare different types of metamorphoses, consider using butterflies (available at Insect Lore: *www.insectlore.com*). If it is not possible for your classroom to have live specimens, then have pictures available that show insects in different stages of complete and incomplete metamorphosis.

- Students' science notebooks
- Hand lens (one for each pair of students)

Safety Alert: Use plastic gloves for handling egg cases.

When the Lesson Is Over: If the butterflies and praying mantises are noninvasive and/or are native to the area, they can be released into the environment as they are both beneficial insects. Before doing so, however, check with your local county extension agent to be sure of any local ordinances to the contrary.

Engage (5–8)

Animals and plants all go through different stages in their lifetimes. A human goes through four main stages of growth: baby, young child, adolescent, and adult. Most plants go through three stages of growth: seed, sprout, and mature plant. Ask students:

- How do you think insects change during their life cycles? (Try to avoid questions that have a yes or no answer such as "Do insects go through different stages?" These so-called unproductive questions (Worth et al. 2009) almost immediately exclude anyone without that background experience.)
- What insect life cycles have you observed or do you know about?

All insects start out their lives as eggs, but what happens after that depends on the insect and whether it goes through incomplete metamorphosis or complete metamorphosis.

---

* The number of egg cases you order depends on the cost of the egg cases and whether the district or the individual teacher is paying for them. The activity can be done as a classroom demonstration with only one egg case (in a terrarium); in groups of three to five students with each group having its own terrarium and egg case; or—in an ideal world—with each student having his or her own terrarium and egg case.

Explore (5–8)

Guiding Question: How does a praying mantis change as it grows?

1. Have each of the student groups examine the praying mantis egg case(s) and record their observations. (*Caution:* Students must wear plastic gloves for this part of the activity.)

2. Ask the students to predict the life stages the praying mantis will go through.

3. In each group, students create an observation chart as they watch the egg hatch and the nymph (baby mantis) develop. They should also predict when they think the eggs will hatch.

4. After the praying mantises have hatched from the eggs and changed from nymphs to adults, students make charts on which they compare the incomplete metamorphosis of the praying mantis with the complete metamorphosis of another insect, such as a butterfly.

Building Student Understanding (K–4 and 5–8)

This part of the lesson can be used with either primary or intermediate grade students by adapting various questions to the appropriate grade level. As students gain practice with the see-scan-analyze thinking process (Figure 6.1), they will need less and less guidance. In the meantime, to facilitate the conversation and prompt students' thinking, you may want to have lists of questions on hand to guide the discussion. The following three lists of questions are not designed as an interrogation, nor do you have to ask each question. They are just prompts to initiate the discussion. They can be used at different grade-level spans, depending on the students' cognitive abilities.

Figure 6.1 See-Scan-Analyze Thinking Process

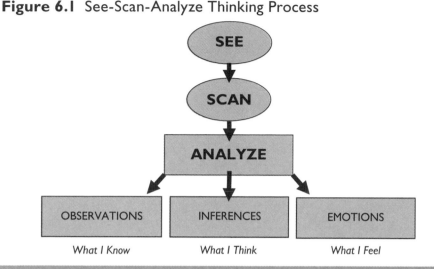

Gathering Observable Information

Have students observe the picture of a praying mantis in Figure 6.2 (p. 72). Here are some questions you might ask after they look at the picture:

- What do you observe about the animal?
- What shape does the head have?
- What do you notice about its legs? Are they all the same? How are they different?
- What is the animal standing on?
- Does it have observable wings?
- How would you describe the head? Does the head have a certain shape?
- What do you notice about the head? Can you observe any eyes?
- How many different body sections can you see?

Making Inferences

- Where do you think this animal might be found?
- How could it catch its food? What type of things might it eat?
- Can you demonstrate how you think it moves?
- Do you think it ever flies? If so, how? Where are its wings?

Figure 6.2 Praying Mantis

Source: SXC.hu, HAAP Media Ltd.

- What other colors do you think the praying mantis might be?
- What might the two things on its head be used for?
- How do you think this animal sees?
- What do you think the pointed parts on the front legs are used for?

Questions Students Are Likely to Ask

The kinds of questions that students ask will depend on their own prior experiences with praying mantises. Here are some possible questions:

- What is it called?
- Where could I see one outside?
- Does it bite or sting?
- It is a helpful or harmful insect?
- How big is it in real life?

Students in the primary grades will focus more on the observable characteristics of the praying mantis than on making inferences.

Reading a Diagram and Making a Model (K–4 and 5–8)

In this section, we take students from a photograph of an insect (Figure 6.2) to a diagram (illustration) of that insect (Figure 6.3) and then to the construction of their own models of the insect.

Look back at Chapter 3—especially pages 26–29. What type of information is conveyed in a simple illustration or diagram? Students should ask the same questions they asked in Chapter 3 (p. 29) in order to analyze and make meaning from Figure 6.3.

- Are there words in this diagram that I don't understand or that are new to me? (Example: the term *thorax* as a section of the body)
- How is the diagram organized? Is it organized in a way that helps me understand new information? (Example: the parts of the praying mantis)

Figure 6.3 Praying Mantis (Labeled Diagram)

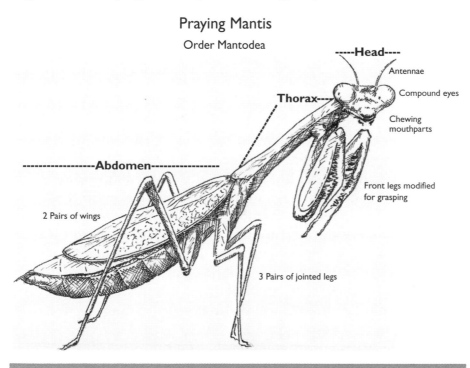

Source: Illustration by Michael Biewener. Reprinted with permission.

- Does the diagram show how parts of the object fit together and how they are related to one another? (Example: the organization, location, and arrangement of the body parts)
- Does the diagram show something that I might not usually see or that is usually hidden from view? (No example in this particular diagram)
- Does the diagram depict the actual size of the subject, or does it show the size of the parts in relation to something else, or does it contain no proportional-size relationships? (All body parts are in proportion to one another; this diagram represents an average-size praying mantis.)

The information presented to the students in Figure 6.3 sets up the academic language they will need to further their understanding of the concept (the structure and parts of organisms). The words and the diagram work together to help students make meaning of the various body parts of the praying mantis. The students have already been drawn into the learning process by the photograph (Figure 6.2); now the diagram (Figure 6.3) provides a visual representation of the labeled parts of a praying mantis. (The teacher may want to have younger students place the photograph and the diagram side-by-side to help them see the relationship between the two. Not having many experiences to draw on, younger students rely heavily on discussing the similarities and differences between the images the teacher shows them.)

Students should have been recording information in their science notebooks and making a drawing of the praying mantis. Now, based on their visual experiences with two different types of graphic illustrations—a photograph and a labeled diagram—older students are ready to create their own models (e.g., a three-dimensional graphic organizer). "With the development of spatial models, or three-dimensional graphic organizers, the students can now take their learning to the next cognitive level, as this representation is a predecessor to full-fledged modeling" (Michaels, Shouse, and Schweingruber 2008, p. 87). Lehrer and Schauble (2006) observed a characteristic shift in the understanding of modeling over the span of elementary and middle school. These researchers developed a learning progression that emphasized different and increasingly complex ideas in different grade bands.

Recomposing New Information

Nonlinguistic representations are one of the nine instructional strategies identified by Marzano, Pickering, and Pollack (2001) that affect student achievement. Research also shows that nonlinguistic representations need two critical attributes to be successful: explicit engagement in and creation by the viewer (Gerlic and Jausovec 1999). The conscious process of storing information begins once the brain chooses to pay attention to the information that has emotion or meaning attached to it. At this stage in the learning sequence, students need to process this information into their working memories. It is therefore necessary for them to consciously "chunk" information together—in other words, they must "recompose" the information; otherwise the working memory will be overloaded and the information will be lost (Hyerle 2004, p. 30). Having the students create their own three-dimensional graphic organizers can be a useful form of assessment (either formative or summative).

The synthesis of visual tools can occur in any phase of the learning sequence depending on the objective for the synthesis. The teacher must ask him- or herself these questions:

- What is the outcome I hope to achieve with these tools?
- How will the use of the tools help my students demonstrate understanding of their new knowledge?
- Would a diagram or an illustration be more useful than a graphic organizer?
- Will the tools—that is, the three-dimensional graphic organizers and thinking maps—be used as summative or formative assessment tools or as study guides for independent review?

Throughout the learning sequence, students will record and draw in their science notebooks. The visual and spatial tools can be placed directly into their notebooks to act as another vehicle for helping them understand—and internalize this understanding of—the concept.

An example of a student's recomposition of the information he has learned is shown in Figure 6.4 (a thinking map) (p. 76). Figures 6.5a, 6.5b, 6.6a, 6.6b, 6.7a, and 6.7b (all three-dimensional graphic organizers or "foldables") show other ways to recompose information. See Chapter 5 for more information on three-dimensional graphic organizers.

CHAPTER 6

Professional Learning Communities

If you are working in a professional learning community, it is time for you to work with your partners to practice using the visual literacy tools that were shown in this chapter. You might choose to write a lesson that fits your learning objectives and then develop the different stages of the 5E Instructional Model (Engage, Explore, Explain, Elaborate, and Evaluate) using the visual literacy models that have been provided.

Figure 6.4 Praying Mantis (Tree Diagram)

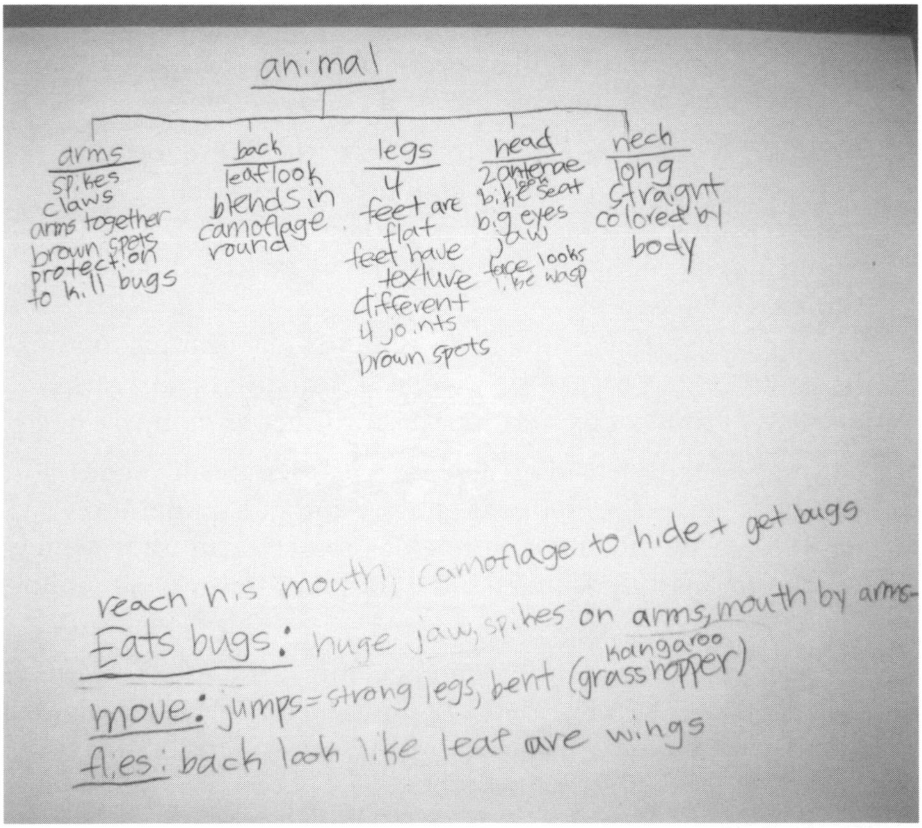

Figure 6.5a Praying Mantis (Three-Tab Foldable, closed)

Figure 6.5b Praying Mantis's Thorax (Three-Tab Foldable, open)

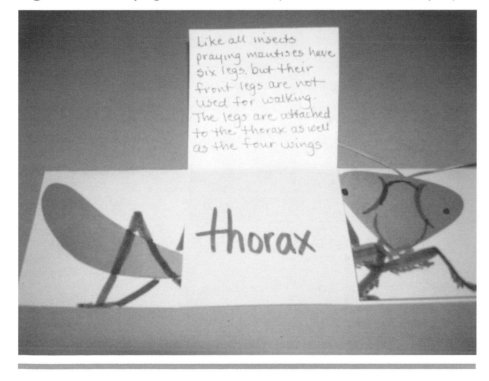

Like all insects praying mantises have six legs. but their front legs are not used for walking. The legs are attached to the thorax as well as the four wings

thorax

The foldables pictured on pages 77, 78, and 79 were constructed for use in this book by Frankie Troutman, a veteran elementary school teacher and one of the authors of the book. These visual literacy tools are normally constructed in the classroom by students.

CHAPTER 6

Figure 6.6a Praying Mantis (Incomplete Metamorphosis, closed)

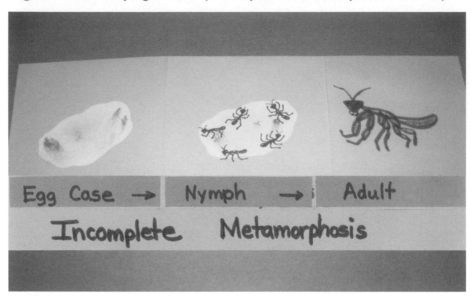

Figure 6.6b Praying Mantis, Nymph Stage (Incomplete Metamorphosis, open)

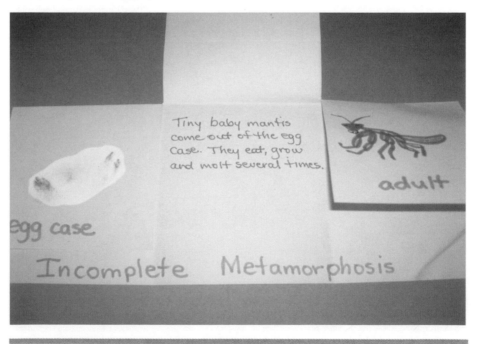

Figure 6.7a Lady Bug (Four Stages of Complete Metamorphosis, closed)

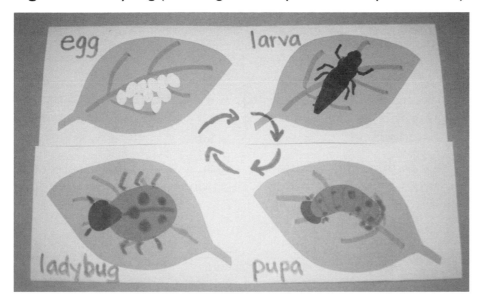

Figure 6.7b Lady Bug (Four Stages of Complete Metamorphosis, open to show larva stage description)

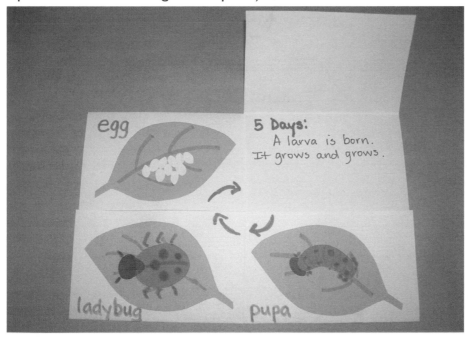

Grades K–4, Organisms and Their Environments, and Grades 5–8, Populations and Ecosystems

Objectives

K–4: Students will be able to identify the roles of different organisms in a food web.

5–8: Students will recognize that food chains overlap with one another in order to form a more complex pattern called a food web.

Depending on your students' grade level, choose an objective and write down some questions you would ask—and students are likely to ask—about the picture in Figure 6.8. See pages 71–72 for examples of each type of question.

*Objective:*_____

Gathering Observable Information

1. _____

2. _____

3. _____

4. _____

5. _____

Making Inferences

1. _____

2. _____

3. _____

4. _____

5. _____

CHAPTER 6

80

Figure 6.8 Eagle (Predator) With Fish (Prey)

Source: SXC.hu, HAAP Media Ltd.

Questions Students Are Likely to Ask

1. _____

2. _____

3. _____

4. _____

5. _____

Figure 6.9 illustrates a pond food web. Think about this web and how the flow of information is being depicted. Keep in mind the appropriate learning objectives for your grade level. Think back to the discussion in Chapter 3 (where we first saw this diagram, on p. 35) about different types of diagrams and consider the inherent difficulties students might have with this type of visual.

CHAPTER 6

Figure 6.9 A Pond Food Web

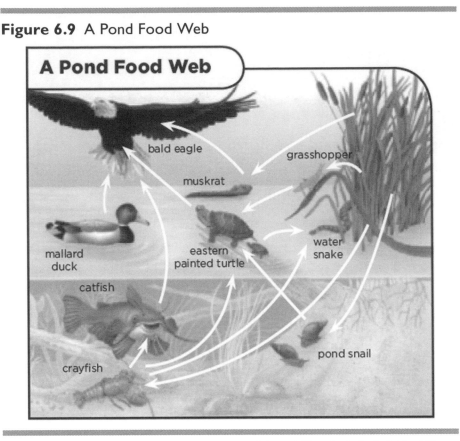

Then write some questions you would ask about this diagram.

1. _____

2. _____

3. _____

4. _____

5. _____

Now is the time for you to decide which of the graphic organizers and thinking maps you would use to help your students re-compose their new knowledge. As part of this learning progression, you can incorporate the use of science notebooks and other visual literacy tools.

CHAPTER 7
Visual Literacy in Earth Science:
Phases of the Moon

"'Would you tell me, please, which way I ought to go from here?' said Alice.

'That depends a good deal on where you want to get to,' said the Cat."

—Lewis Carroll, *Alice's Adventures in Wonderland*
(1865)

When designing Earth science visual literacy tools, students and teachers must think first about the content being expressed and then how they will construct meaning from this content. Spatial thinking uses representations to help us remember, understand, and communicate about the properties of objects, whether or not those objects themselves are inherently spatial. In the teaching and learning of Earth science concepts, many visual representations can be complex, ranging from a cross section of a volcano to a geologic time sequence showing the formation of a mountain. Because of this complexity, diagrams and other visual images can become critical visual literacy tools. As you proceed through the following exercises, think about the Earth science lessons you are currently using and the content knowledge your students need to know. Also think of the visual literacy tools you can use to help them learn that knowledge.

MEETING THE STANDARD

K–4 *Changes in the Earth and Sky:* Objects in the sky have patterns of movement….The moon moves across the sky on a daily basis much like the sun. The observable shape of the moon changes from day to day in a cycle that lasts about a month. (p. 135)

National Science Education Standards (NRC 1996), Content Standard D: Earth and Space Science

Grades K–4, Changes in the Earth and Sky

Objective (K–4)

The student will be able to describe and illustrate how the Moon appears to change shape over a period of time (one month).

Purpose (K–4)

This activity will give students the opportunity to make and record their own observations of the Moon during the course of one month. The students will match their observations of the Moon phases with experiences they have had observing the Moon at other times and will be able to discuss the changing phases of the Moon.

"Phases of the Moon"
Teacher Background for Grades K–4 and 5–8*

The Moon revolves around Earth, and Earth revolves around the Sun. When we look at the Moon, it appears to change shape. Actually, the Moon's shape is always the same. What does change is the amount of the Moon's lit side that we can see. The Moon reflects the Sun's light; it has no light of its own. So, "moonlight" is actually reflected sunlight.

It takes 27.3 days for the Moon to *revolve* around, or *orbit,* the Earth. It takes the same amount of time for the Moon to *rotate* or spin on its axis. This causes the same side of the Moon to be facing Earth at all times. The "dark" side of the Moon, the side facing away from Earth, has been photographed only from spacecraft.

The stages in the predictable, repeating Moon cycle are known as Moon *phases.* During the *new Moon* phase, the Moon is between the Sun and the Earth. At that time, because the lit side of the Moon faces away from Earth, we cannot see the Moon (even though it is called the "new" Moon).

_____

* "Research reveals that students have many misconceptions about the Moon. One of the most common misconceptions is that Moon phases are caused by Earth's shadow falling on the Moon. Students may also incorrectly believe that clouds covering the Moon cause the Moon's phases, that the Moon has a face, and that the Moon can only be seen at night" (Ansberry and Morgan 2010, p. 249).

Source: Moon images licensed under the Creative Commons Attribution 3.0 Unported/GNU Free Documentation License.

Next, in the *waxing* [growing] *phases*, the lit side of the Moon becomes more and more visible. ("Light on the right, the Moon is getting bright.") If we see less than half of the Moon lit on the right, we are seeing a *waxing crescent moon*. When we see the entire right half of the waxing Moon, we are seeing a *first-quarter moon*. As the Moon continues to orbit Earth, more than half of the side facing Earth becomes visible. The Moon in this phase is called a *waxing gibbous Moon* (*gibbous* means rounded and bulging).

Finally, the Moon reaches the opposite side of its orbit, and its entire lit side faces Earth. When its entire lit side becomes visible, what we are seeing is called a *full Moon*. The period from the new Moon to the full Moon is about 14.5 days.

After the full Moon, we see less and less of the Moon's lit side. The Moon is then in its *waning phases* (*waning* means becoming less). The first phase to appear is the *waning gibbous moon*. This phase is followed by the *third-quarter moon*—the left half of the lit side is visible. The next phase is the *waning crescent moon*, which decreases until the Moon is no longer visible at all—the new Moon phase. The waning phases take about 14.5 days. Our whole concept of a month comes from the length of the cycle of phases of the Moon, which is about 29.5 days.

These two websites offer additional information about the Moon and its phases:

1. U.S. Naval Observatory, Naval Oceanography Portal:
    www.usno.navy.mil/USNO/astronomical-applications

    This excellent site offers complete Sun and Moon data for any day and any area in the United States. This information gives all students, especially younger ones and those who have little parental support, an equal opportunity to participate in the Moon observations. Also, having access to this daily information means that when nights are too cloudy to see the Moon or when the moonrise time is past the students' bedtimes, students will still be able to fill in their calendars. This site even has a time-lapse movie of the Moon during March and April 1998. The movie clearly shows a complete cycle of the Moon's phases.

2. National Science Digital Library:
    http://NSDL.org

Topic: Moon Phases
    (K–4)
Go to: *www.scilinks.org*
Code: DVL001

Topic: Moon Phases
    (5–8)
Go to: *www.scilinks.org*
Code: DVL002

Materials (K–4)

- One blank calendar chart for each student to be used to record the Moon's shapes throughout the month with perhaps another week added. (It is a good idea to include the extra days so that students observe the crescent Moon after the new Moon; some students think that the phases back up instead of starting over.)

Engage (K–4)

Begin by asking the following questions:

- What do you see when you look up at the sky at night and look for the Moon?
- How does the position and shape of the Moon appear to change over the course of a few nights? A week? A month? Use pictures and words to tell about what shapes you saw when you looked at the Moon.

Explore (K–4)

Guiding Question: How does the Moon's shape appear to change throughout the month?

1. Distribute a blank calendar chart to each student. Tell students to record the shape of the Moon they see in the night sky every night for the next four weeks. Encourage them to have their families participate with them in these observations. (See the remarks about the U.S. Naval Observatory's website—*www. usno.navy.mil/USNO/astronomical-applications*—on p. 85 regarding this step. The daily information on this site will be needed when nights are too cloudy to see the Moon or when the moonrise time is past the students' bedtimes.)

2. Every day for the next four weeks, have the students report in class on the Moon's shape for the night before. Have them draw their observations on the board. While they are doing these drawings, talk about how the Moon's shape is changing and provide familiar names for the Moon's different shapes or phases (see pp. 84–85). *Ask:* Is there ever a time when there seems to be no Moon in the sky?

3. Primary age students are very interested in basic Moon facts— for example, that the Moon is smaller than the Earth, that it has no light of its own but reflects light from the Sun, that there is no air or water on the Moon, and that it revolves around the Earth. The fact that the Moon has phases, and the names of those phases, will probably be new and interesting to them.

4. Third and fourth graders will want to review and discuss the basic facts and vocabulary about the phases of the Moon.

Grades 5–8, Earth in the Solar System

Objective (5–8)
The student will identify the phases of the Moon and explain why these phases occur.

Purpose (5–8)
Sometimes the Moon appears perfectly round. At other times it looks like a small crescent or even seems to disappear. To learn why this is, students will create a model of how the position of the Moon changes in relation to the Sun and to Earth.

Materials (5–8)
- Three balls of different sizes (e.g., blown-up beach ball, tennis ball, and Ping-Pong ball). It would be ideal if each student group of five or six students could have a set of the three balls.
- Black marker
- Science notebook for each student

Engage (5–8)
Begin by asking the following questions:

- How does the Moon's shape appear to change?
- How would you describe the different changing shapes of the Moon that you have seen?
- Do you think the Moon itself actually changes shape or does it just appear to us on Earth to change?
- Do you have any ideas as to why the Moon appears to change its shape?

> **MEETING THE STANDARD**
>
> *5–8 Earth in the Solar System:* Most objects in the solar system are in regular and predictable motion. Those motions explain such phenomena as the day, the year, phases of the moon, and eclipses. (p. 160)
>
> *National Science Education Standards* (NRC 1996), Content Standard D: Earth and Space Science

CHAPTER 7

Explore (5–8)

Guiding Question: What causes the Moon's shape to appear to change?

To the Student:

1. To make a model, you will need three balls of different sizes (*Teacher: see Materials list*), which will represent the Sun, the Moon, and Earth. Place the largest ball, representing the Sun, in one location. Take the smallest ball, representing the Moon, darken one-half of it with a marker, and place it several inches from the Sun. The medium-size ball represents the Earth. Place it several inches from the Moon. Move the Moon around the Earth, making sure that the white (sunlit) side of the Moon is always facing the Sun. The dark (unlit) side should always face away from the Sun. *Why is it necessary to have the lit side of the Moon facing the Sun?*

2. With a partner, arrange the model of the Earth, the Sun, and the Moon in such a way that someone on Earth would see a full Moon. Make a diagram of the locations of the Sun, Moon, and Earth in your model. Label your diagram.

3. Draw and label the different Moon phases: first-quarter Moon, full Moon, third-quarter Moon, new Moon, waxing crescent Moon.

Building Student Understanding (K–4 and 5–8)

Figure 7.1 See-Scan-Analyze Thinking Process

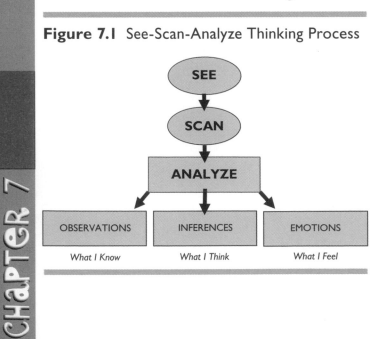

This part of the lesson can be used with either primary or intermediate grade students by adapting various questions to the appropriate grade level. As students gain practice with the see-scan-analyze thinking process (Figure 7.1), they will need less and less guidance. In the meantime, to facilitate the conversation and prompt students' thinking, you may want to have some questions on hand. The following lists of questions regarding Figure 7.2 are not designed as an interrogation, nor do you have to ask every one of them. They are just prompts to initiate the discussion.

Figure 7.2 Moon Rising Behind a House

Source: SXC.hu, HAAP Media Ltd.

Gathering Observable Information

- Where is the Moon in this picture?
- How would you describe the Moon's appearance?
- Where is the Moon in relation to the house?
- What do you notice about the trees in the picture?
- What do you notice about the house in the picture?

Making Inferences (See answers on pp. 97–98.)

- Why does the Moon appear white?
- The Moon appears to have dark spots on its surface. What might those be?
- Why is the house lighter than the trees? Where do you think the light is coming from?
- Is it nighttime or daytime? What makes you think this?
- At what time of year might this picture have been taken?

Questions Students Are Likely to Ask (See answers on pp. 98–99.)

The kinds of questions that students generate will depend on their own prior experiences. Here are some possible student questions:

- Why does the Moon in the photograph look so big?
- Why does the Moon seem to get smaller as it goes higher into the sky at night?
- Why aren't there any stars?
- There are times when there is no Moon in the sky. Where does it go?

Remember that students in the primary grades will focus more on the observable characteristics of the objects in the photograph than on making inferences. They may not have had many prior experiences to draw on regarding the sky at night.

Reading a Diagram and Illustration

(*Students need to be familiar with the phases of the Moon as discussed on pp. 84–85 in order to work with Figure 7.3.*)

The synthetic diagram of the Moon's orbit in Figure 7.3 provides a visual and verbal connection for the students. As you will remember from Chapter 3, synthetic diagrams (pp. 29–37) are illustrations that make connections between parts of a sequence or that link subgroups together within a larger group. They often use arrows or numbers to make the connections apparent to the viewer. In Figure 7.3, the synthetic diagram is used to demonstrate how the Moon revolves around Earth and the differing views of the sun-lit portion of the Moon's surface as seen by an Earth observer at those positions.

Let's analyze the diagram in Figure 7.3.

- Does the illustration show the Sun?
- In which direction do you read the diagram? Why do you think the arrows go in this direction?
- What do the dotted lines signify in the diagram?
- How do the photos of the Moon relate to the drawings of the Moon? Are they showing the same thing or a different perspective? How can you tell?
- How does this diagram help show the different positions of the Moon throughout its revolution around Earth?

Figure 7.3 Synthetic Diagram of the Moon's Orbit

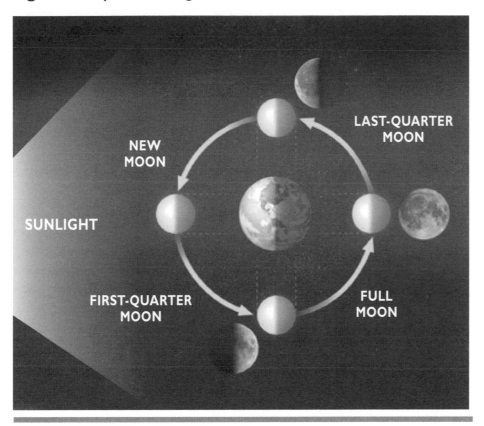

Source: Adapted from Hackett, J. K., R. H. Moyer, and J. Vasquez. 2008. *Science A Closer Look.* Grade 6, Visual Literacy. Columbus, OH: Macmillan/McGraw-Hill. Copyright © 2008 Macmillan/McGraw-Hill. Reprinted with permission.

- There are only three actual Moon photographs, but there are four drawings representing the Moon. Why are there only three photographs?
- How does this diagram illustrate why we do not see the new Moon phase?

The linear diagram of the phases of the Moon in Figure 7.4 (p. 92) provides the students with a different, more complex visual representation from the one in Figure 7.3. Some students might look at this linear diagram and mistakenly assume that all of the photos were taken on the same night. It is important for students

CHAPTER 7

Figure 7.4 Linear Diagram Showing the Moon's Phases

to recognize that the linear diagram in Figure 7.4 is a compilation of photos taken over the course of a month. Also, this diagram does not include arrows to direct the viewer's attention or to indicate that it shows a sequence of events. The viewer must deduce that these are multiple views of the same object (the Moon) and that the figure is depicting a succession of visual changes.

It is also important to remind students that the viewer's position is stationary in this diagram. The sunlight reflecting off the surface of the Moon changes during the course of the cycle of the Moon.

Both the synthetic diagram of the Moon's orbit (Figure 7.3) and the linear diagram of the phases of the Moon (Figure 7.4) help students visualize the critical concept of the changing phases of the Moon. The synthetic diagram illustrates how the Moon appears to change as it revolves around the Earth. The linear diagram provides a visual representation of the different phases as the Moon transitions from one phase to another. These visual images can make information in textbooks about the Moon's orbit and phases a lot easier to understand.

Recomposing New Information

The next cognitive level in any lesson such as this one is the *synthesis* of the visual tools, which happens when the students recompose their new knowledge into spatial representations and visual thinking tools. These visual thinking tools can be used in any phase of the learning sequence depending on the teacher's objectives.

Before deciding which tools to use, the teacher should ask him- or herself the following questions:

- What is the outcome I hope to achieve with these tools?
- How will the use of these tools help my students demonstrate understanding of their new knowledge?
- Will these tools be used as summary tools, as assessment tools, or as study guides for independent review?

Throughout the learning sequence, students will be recording and drawing in their science notebooks. Their visual and spatial tools can be placed directly into their notebooks to act as another vehicle for helping them understand the concept and internalize that understanding.

The students are now ready to synthesize their learning with their own graphic representations. Examples of students' work in which they have recomposed the information they learned are shown in Figures 7.5a, 7.5b, and 7.5c.

Figure 7.5a Moon Phases (Cycle Format)

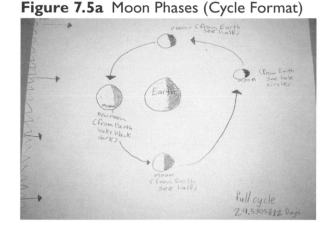

Figure 7.5b Moon Phases (Linear Format)

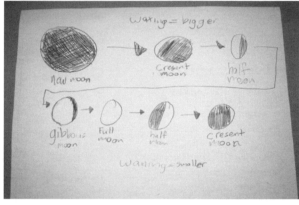

Figure 7.5c New Moon and Full Moon Attributes (Venn Diagram)

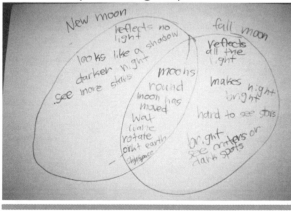

CHAPTER 7

Figure 7.6 Moon Phases (Accordion Foldable, open)

Grades 5–8, Structure of the Earth System

Objective

5–8 The student will be able to demonstrate through visuals and concrete materials how fault-block mountains can be formed.

Decide what questions you would ask—and students are likely to ask—about the picture in Figure 7.8. See pages 89–90 for examples of each type of question.

Objective: _____

Gathering Observable Information

1. _____

2. _____

3. _____

4. _____

5. _____

The foldables on this page and on the top of page 95 were constructed for use in this book by Frankie Troutman, a veteran elementary school teacher and one of the authors of the book. These visual literacy tools are normally constructed in the classroom by students.

Figure 7.7a Moon Phases
(Envelope Foldable, closed)

Figure 7.7b Moon Phases
(Envelope Foldable, open)

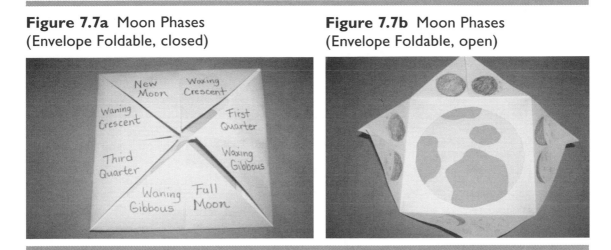

Making Inferences

1. _____

2. _____

3. _____

4. _____

5. _____

Figure 7.8 Fault-Block Mountains

Source: Photo by Jack Sanders, Mesa, AZ. Reprinted with permission.

CHAPTER 7

Questions Students Are Likely to Ask

1. _____

2. _____

3. _____

4. _____

5. _____

Reading the Diagram

Figure 7.9 illustrates three different types of faults. Think about the diagram and how the flow of information is being depicted. Keep in mind the appropriate learning objective for your grade level. Think back to Chapter 3, in which you learned about different types of diagrams, and consider the difficulties students might have with the illustration in Figure 7.9. Then write some questions you would ask about this diagram.

1. _____

2. _____

3. _____

4. _____

5. _____

Now is the time for you to decide which of the graphic organizers and thinking maps you would use to help your students recompose their new knowledge. As part of this learning progression, you can incorporate the use of science notebooks and other visual literacy tools.

Figure 7.9 Diagram Showing Three Types of Faults

A strike-slip fault is produced at a transform boundary.

A reverse fault is produced at a convergent boundary.

A normal fault is produced at a divergent boundary.

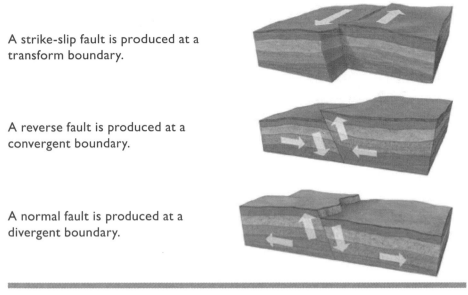

Source: Hackett, J. K., R. H. Moyer, and J. Vasquez. 2008. *Science A Closer Look.* Grade 6, Visual Literacy. Columbus, OH: Macmillan/McGraw-Hill, p. 39. Copyright © 2008 Macmillan/McGraw-Hill. Reprinted with permission.

Answers to Questions on Pages 89–90

Making Inferences

Q: Why does the Moon appear white?

A: The Sun's light is reflecting off the dusty and rocky surface of the Moon, giving it the whitish color we see.

Q: The Moon appears to have dark spots on its surface. What might those be?

A: The dark spots are huge impact basins (commonly called "craters") that were flooded with now-solidified lava. The maria (or "seas" as the ancient astronomers called them) are darker than the surrounding areas because the rock is basalt (a volcanic rock that is darker than the material making up the mountains surrounding it).

(continued on page 98)

CHAPTER 7

("Making Inferences" continued from page 97)

Q: Why is the house lighter than the trees? Where do you think the light is coming from?

A: The upper portions of the house are reflecting some sunlight. The trees may be in the shadow of something not seen in the picture, maybe other trees, thus making them look darker than the house.

Q: Is it nighttime or daytime? What makes you think this?

A: It is sunset—the sunlight reaching the upper levels of the house indicates that the Sun is nearly at the horizon.

Q: At what time of year might this picture have been taken?

A: In the fall. The leaves are gone from the taller trees yet there appear to still be some leaves on the small bush near the house. Also, the grasses in the foreground are still tall.

Questions Students Are Likely to Ask

Q: Why does the Moon in the photograph look so big?

A: This is called the Moon illusion. It is an optical illusion in which the Moon appears larger near the horizon than it does when higher up in the sky. The illusion that the Moon is larger on the horizon is caused by perspective—you compare the Moon with other objects (like trees or buildings) that are closer to you. Measure the Moon's size against something held at arm's length when it is rising. Wait two hours and measure it again. You will find that despite the Moon looking vast on the horizon, it is still the same size when it is higher in the sky.

(continued on page 99)

("Questions Students Are Likely to Ask" continued from page 98)

Q: Why does the Moon seem to get smaller as it goes higher into the sky at night?

A: See previous answer.

Q: Why aren't there any stars?

A: The amount of sunlight at this time of evening is still too bright and prevents us from seeing the stars.

Q: There are times when there is no Moon in the sky. Where does it go?

A: The Moon is always in the sky in orbit around the Earth. We just don't see it during the new Moon phase because the side of the Moon that is facing us is not being lit by the Sun. The Moon also rises a bit later every day and sets a bit later and is sometimes below the horizon where it can't be seen. The only time it is visible all night long is on the night of the full Moon, which occurs approximately once a month.

CHAPTER 7

CHAPTER 8
Visual Literacy in Physical Science: Force and Motion

A few years before his death, Albert Einstein was describing the process of science to a lifelong friend, Maurice Solovine, who, though not a scientist (he was a philosopher and mathematician), enjoyed discussing science. According to the often-told story, Solovine was very confused and had trouble understanding what Einstein was talking about. It was only when Einstein pulled out a pen and drew an illustration with words to explain his thinking that Solovine understood—he "saw" what Einstein was trying to say.

Like Maurice Solovine, most of us have trouble visualizing certain concepts because they are very complicated. We might hear or read the words that describe an idea, but it is only when we see them drawn or sketched in a visual form that we begin to understand them. Suppose, for example, that you are trying to explain to students what happens when a ball is thrown into the air and gravitational force acts on it, pulling it back to Earth. Although students cannot see this force, diagrams and pictures can provide a visual representation of what is happening. Once your students become visually literate, like Einstein, they will be able to show what is happening in their investigations through the creation of their own visual images.

Topic: What Are
    Forces? (K–4)
Go to: *www.scilinks.org*
Code: DVL003

Topic: Forces and
    Motion (K–4)
Go to: *www.scilinks.org*
Code: DVL004

Grades K–4, Position and Motion of Objects*

Objective (K–4)

The student will be able to observe how the amount of force affects an object's motion.

Purpose (K–4)

The student will observe how different amounts of force affect how an object moves.

Materials (K–4)

- Masking tape for "starting lines"
- Science notebook for each student
- For each group of three students:
  - One toy car
  - One ruler

Plan ahead: Set up the masking-tape starting lines on the floor around the classroom. Space the starting lines so that each group has enough space to work.

Engage (K–4)

Begin by asking the following questions:

- When have you made something move?
- If your friend is on a swing and she asks you to help her swing, what do you do?
- If you want to make a ball go into the air, what do you have to do? (Objects cannot start to move on their own. They need to have a push or a pull to put them in motion. This push or pull on an object is called a *force*.)
- Think of how you open a drawer. What kind of force do you need?

Explore (K–4)

Guiding Question: How can you make objects go farther and faster?

1. Begin by asking the students to describe the different ways they think they can make the toy cars move. Have them demonstrate these movements and then explain that they are going to do an investigation to see how they can make their cars move even farther and faster.

---

*"The topic of force and motion presents difficult challenges for both students and their teachers. Students have had more direct, personal experience with the ideas of force and motion than with perhaps any other topic in the science curriculum; thus, they often come to class with fully formed and strongly held beliefs. Not all of these beliefs are consistent with a scientific view, however" (Keeley and Harrington 2010, p. 1). For help in determining what preconceptions about force and motion your students may bring to the classroom, see Page Keeley and Rand Harrington's recent book, *Uncovering Student Ideas in Physical Science, Volume 1: 45 New Force and Motion Assessment Probes.*

"Force and Motion"

Teacher Background for Grades K–4 and 5–8

What do you think makes something move? You know from your own observations that objects cannot start to move on their own but require a push or a pull to put them into motion. When you kick a soccer ball to move it across the field, your kick is a push. If you do not kick the ball, it will stay in the same place. If you push something, it will move away from you. If you pull it, it will move toward you. A push or pull is called a *force*.

When you swim, you know that you must push and pull harder against the water to swim faster. When you run, you push harder against the ground than when you walk. The size of the force affects an object's *acceleration* (a rate of change of velocity as a function of time). A larger force gives the object more acceleration.

The *mass* of an object matters, too. If you apply the same force to an object with less mass, that object accelerates more than an object with greater mass. If you are trying to pull a load in a wagon, your pull will cause the wagon to accelerate. If you get someone to help you pull the same load, then the acceleration will be greater. Why? Because two people exert more force than one person. What would happen if the load you have to pull were twice as large and you pulled with the same force as you did before? Then the load would accelerate only half as much.

Source: Images provided by gbh007 for iStockphoto.

2. To do this investigation, each group lines up its car at the starting line. One student in each group gently pushes the car over the starting line. Each group then measures how far its car rolled. Discuss with the students the different distances the cars rolled. Why do they think there might have been a difference in the distances? How can they make the cars roll farther?

3. Have the students conduct several runs with their cars. They should record each distance rolled in their science notebooks. With younger students who have not been introduced to rulers, use different pieces of string cut to certain lengths that they can lay out on the floor.

CHAPTER 8

4. Discuss with students why some cars went farther than others. Discuss the term *force*—the cars that went farther had a greater amount of force acting on them.

Grades 5–8, Motions and Forces

Objective (5–8)

The student will be able to explain that the motion of an object can be described by its position, direction, and speed.

Purpose (5–8)

This activity will help students recognize that speed is a function of both distance and time. To find out how fast something is moving, they measure the distance the object travels and the length of time it needed to travel that distance.

Materials (5–8)

For each group of three students:

- One windup toy (One source for windup toys is Office Playground, Inc., 83 Hamilton Drive, Ste. 100, Novato, CA 94949-5674. *www.officeplayground.com.* 800-458-1948.
- Masking tape (for "starting lines")
- Stopwatch or watch with second hand
- Meterstick
- Calculator
- Science notebook for each student

Engage (5–8)

Describe what you see when you watch two people racing along on bicycles.

- How can you tell that they are moving? (Possible answer: Their positions/locations changed from one moment to the next.)
- How could you measure how fast they are traveling? (Possible answer: Determine how far they went and how long it took them to get from the starting line to the finish line.)
- How would you compare who is faster if they raced at different times? (Possible answer: Compare the speed of one racer to the speed of the other.)

By knowing where something starts and how long it takes to travel a certain distance, we can determine how fast something moves. In this lesson, we will explore how to measure how fast things move.

Explore (5–8)

Guiding Question: How can you tell how fast things move?

Put students into groups of four. Instruct each group to do the following:

1. Place a long piece of masking tape on a smooth surface. This is your starting line.

2. Give one member of your group a stopwatch. When the windup toy is released, he or she will call out each time a 5-second interval occurs. Another group member will make a mark on the ground at every 5-second interval. The other group members will record in their science notebooks how far the toy moves every 5 seconds until it has gone 30 cm.

3. Wind up the windup toy. Place it at the edge of the starting line and let it go.

4. Carry out step #2 (recording how far the toy moves every 5 seconds) while the toy is moving.

5. When the toy comes to a stop, measure *how far* it went (did it travel the full 30 cm?) and record that information in your science notebook. Also record *how long* it took the toy to travel 30 cm.

6. Repeat steps #3, 4, and 5 two more times, each time recording the data in your science notebook.

7. For each of the three times you let the car go, make a drawing to show how the toy traveled—maybe in a straight line, in a curved line, or along a zigzag path.

   (*Teacher:* This might lead to a discussion about how the "linear distance" could be shorter than the actual path traveled if the toy moved along a curve. You will want to decide which distance the students should record. The class can then discuss variables and setting up controls. The class can also attempt to define what it means to move a distance.)

8. Make a graph using the data you recorded for the three times you "let the car go."

Ask: How can you determine which toy was the fastest? The slowest? (You measure the speed of an object by knowing how far the object traveled and how long it took to cover that distance.)

The speed of anything will have units of distance and time. In this lesson, the calculation of speed is the distance traveled divided by time. The units would be represented as centimeters per second. Have student groups compare the speed of their windup toys with one another.

As you discuss speed, remember to point out that speed contains both a number and a unit. The student graphs will probably show a curved line. This indicates that the speed of the windup toy in each group was not constant. The students probably observed that the toy did not cover the same distance every 5 seconds. Depending on the grade level, students can investigate the changing speed and be introduced to the concepts of velocity and acceleration. (See explanations of—and student "probes" on—the concepts of velocity and acceleration in Keeley and Harrington 2010, pp. 67–137. The grade range for that book is K–12.)

Building Student Understanding (K–4 and 5–8)

To facilitate the conversation about forces and motion and to prompt the students' thinking, you may want to have a series of questions on hand to guide the discussion. As students gain practice with the see-scan-analyze thinking process (Figure 8.1), they will need less and less guidance. The three lists of questions regarding Figure 8.2 are not designed as an interrogation, nor do you have to ask every question. They are just prompts to initiate the discussion.

Gathering Observable Information

- What do you observe in the picture?
- What do you notice about the cart?
- What is the man who is standing up doing?
- What is the man who is sitting down doing?
- What is different about the man standing and the man sitting?
- Do the people appear to be different ages? How can you tell?

Figure 8.1 See-Scan-Analyze Thinking Process

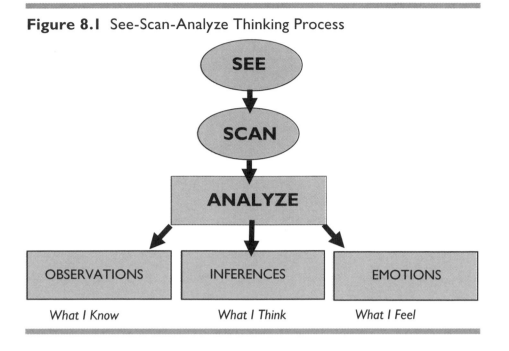

Figure 8.2 Man Pushing Cart With Passengers

Source: Hackett, J. K., R. H. Moyer, and J. Vasquez. 2008. *Science A Closer Look.* Grade 1, Visual Literacy (Student Edition). Columbus, OH: Macmillan/McGraw-Hill, p. 369. Copyright © 2008 Macmillan/McGraw-Hill. Corbis Image. Reprinted with permission.

Making Inferences

- Why does the man who is standing have his hands on the other man's back?
- Do you see any evidence of motion in the picture?
- Why might the man and boy be holding onto the cart?
- Why does the cart have wheels? What would happen if there were no wheels? (Would the cart still move if the man pushed it?)
- How can you tell if the man who is pushing is running or walking?
- What might happen if the man stopped pushing?
- Could the boy push the two men? What would he have to do?
- Why does the older man's hair look like it's blowing?

Questions Students Are Likely to Ask

The different questions that students generate will depend on their own experiences. Their interpersonal responses will be based on their emotional connections to, or prior experiences with, the situation in the picture.

- Is the cart homemade?
- Are they in a race?
- What would happen if only the boy was in the cart and one man was pushing?
- What would happen if both men pushed the boy?

Most students, whether they are primary level or older, will have had some experience riding in a cart or wagon. They will be able to make comments based on their observations and will be able to generate a list of inferences based on their prior experiences. Through this one picture, you can set up the path for learning the K–4 and 5–8 objectives because it captures the concepts of force, motion, push-pull, and acceleration.

Reading Force-and-Motion Diagrams

Figure 8.3 is for primary students and shows the effect of a force on a ball. Figure 8.4 (p. 110) is for intermediate or middle school students and illustrates the effect of force on acceleration. (Recall that Chapter 3 is devoted to various kinds of diagrams.)

Figure 8.3 How a Ball Can Change Directions in a Baseball Game (Arrows indicate direction of the ball.)

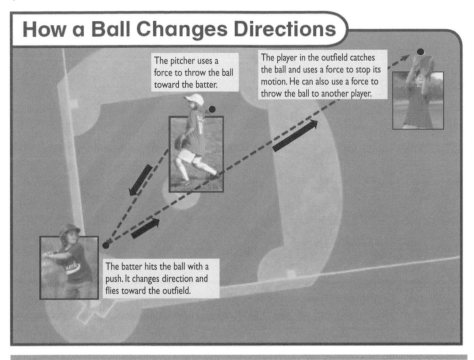

How a Ball Changes Directions

The pitcher uses a force to throw the ball toward the batter.

The player in the outfield catches the ball and uses a force to stop its motion. He can also use a force to throw the ball to another player.

The batter hits the ball with a push. It changes direction and flies toward the outfield.

Source: Hackett, J. K., R. H. Moyer, and J. Vasquez. 2008. *Science A Closer Look.* Grade 2, Visual Literacy. Columbus, OH: Macmillan/McGraw-Hill, p. 33. Copyright © 2008 Macmillan/McGraw-Hill. Reprinted with permission.

Each of the two diagrams has a different function.

1. The diagram in Figure 8.3 shows the flow of information. Students must first look to see where the action begins because the diagram is not cyclical. Once they recognize the starting point, they can begin to follow the information as it "flows" through the diagram, seeing how each player uses forces (push or pull) while playing a game of baseball. The arrows show the directions in which the ball moves because of these forces. The caption next to each picture tells how the force makes the ball move. In this diagram, the captions provide important information necessary to make meaning of the visual images.

Topic: The Science of
Baseball (5–8)
Go to: *www.scilinks.org*
Code: DVL005

Figure 8.4 Relationship of Applied Force and Acceleration

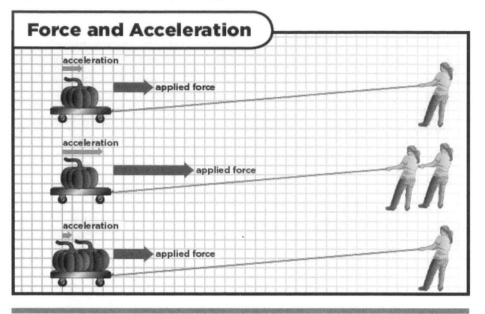

2. In Figure 8.4 the students must recognize that there are three different scenarios being depicted. They must make visual comparisons and determine what makes the scenarios different. There are four items in the diagram that vary: the acceleration arrow (above the pumpkin in each cart); the applied force arrow (in front of each cart); the number of pullers (on the right); and the number of pumpkins in each cart. The background graph grid is important because it helps to indicate "amount" or "strength" as the relative "size" of the arrows for both acceleration and applied force change. Students are able to compare the amount of force applied to the amount of acceleration and have a visual reference check as to the size of the force. By talking through the differences in each scenario, your students will be better able to articulate the changing variables to think about how the application of force and a change in mass can affect acceleration. Once they recognize how the scenarios change, the information provided in the captions will make more sense.

Topic: All About Forces
(5–8)
Go to: *www.scilinks.org*
Code: DVL006

As you observe the two diagrams, compare the different ways that information is being conveyed to the learner. Ask yourself the following questions:

- Would the diagram help my students understand new words (vocabulary) that they might not know, recognize, or understand?
- Does the diagram in Figure 8.3 show how the forces from the players on the field work together to move the ball in different ways? (Example: The pitcher throws the ball, the player hits the ball, and the outfielder catches the ball.)
- If students were to follow the path of the ball in Figure 8.3, would they be able to describe the different forces acting on the ball in order to get it back to the pitcher?
- How will the information presented in Figure 8.4 help the students compare mass, force, and acceleration? What if they do not understand or do not have an operational definition of mass? Would the illustrations of one pumpkin and then two pumpkins help them grasp the concept of mass?
- Does either diagram show something that is not usually seen or that is usually hidden from view?
- Which of the diagrams would I use for the grade level I am teaching? At what point in the 5E Instructional Cycle of my lesson might I use this diagram? Could I use it for more than one purpose?

As you can see, it is the use of images in a diagram, the way the images are organized, and the flow of words in the diagram that work together to help the students make meaning of a concept. In this lesson, the students are drawn into the learning process by the photograph (Figure 8.2), and then the diagrams (Figures 8.3 and 8.4) provide visual representations of the concept.

Recomposing New Information

Students reach a new cognitive level when they can synthesize or recompose new knowledge into spatial representations, such as three-dimensional graphic organizers and other visual literacy tools. Before deciding on which of the tools to use, the teacher should consider these questions:

- What is the outcome I hope to achieve with these tools?
- How will use of the tools help my students demonstrate understanding of their new knowledge?
- Will these tools be used for summative or formative assessment or as study guides for independent review?

Throughout the learning sequence, students will record and draw in their science notebooks. These visual and spatial tools can be placed directly into their notebooks and act as another vehicle for helping them understand—and internalize their understanding of—the concept being studied.

Examples of students recomposing the information they have learned are shown in Figures 8.5a and 8.5b.

The student diagram in Figure 8.5b became a useful formative assessment tool because the student incorrectly stated that the object would accelerate (box 3). When the teacher questioned the student's thinking, the student was able to recognize his error. The visual tool gave the teacher the opportunity to "interview" the student, and the student was able to correct his mistake.

Figure 8.5a Push-Pull (Primary Student)

Figure 8.5b Force and Acceleration (Intermediate Student)

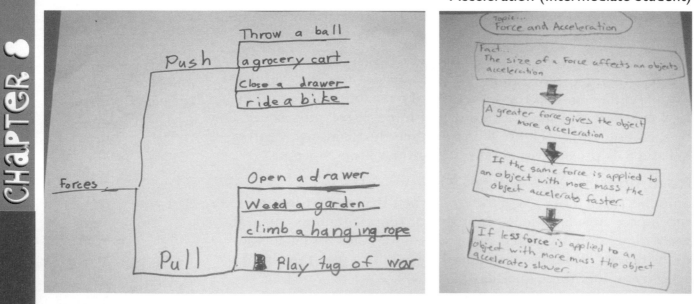

CHAPTER 8

Figure 8.6a
Push-Pull (Matchbook Foldable, closed)

Figure 8.6b
Push-Pull (Matchbook Foldable, open)

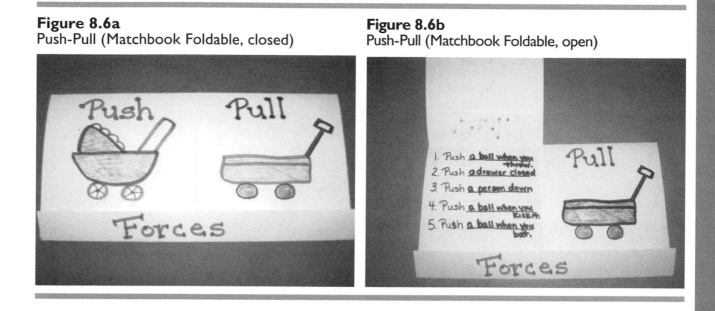

Figure 8.7 Force and Acceleration (Pop-Up/Pop-Out Foldable, open)

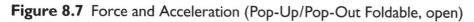
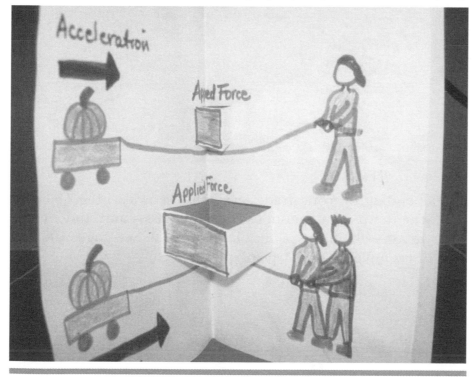

The foldables on this page were constructed for use in this book by Frankie Troutman, a veteran elementary school teacher and one of the authors of the book. These visual literacy tools are normally constructed in the classroom by students.

Grades K–4, Position and Motion of Objects, and Grades 5–8, Motions and Forces

Objectives

K–4: The student will be able to measure and record changes in an object's position.

5–8: The student will be able to compare distance and time.

Figure 8.8 Cheetah Running

Source: SXC.hu, HAAP Media Ltd.

Depending on your grade level, choose a learning objective and write down some questions you would ask—and students are likely to ask—about the picture in Figure 8.8. See pages 106 and 108 for examples of each type of question.

*Objective:*_____

Gathering Observable Information

1. _____

2. _____

3. _____

4. _____

5. _____

Making Inferences

1. _____

2. _____

3. _____

4. _____

5. _____

Questions Students Are Likely to Ask

1. _____

2. _____

3. _____

4. _____

5. _____

CHAPTER 8

Reading the Diagram

The diagram in Figure 8.9 is a graph that depicts the rate of speed of three animals. Keep in mind the appropriate learning objective for your grade level. Write some questions you would ask about this diagram. Think back to Chapter 3, where you learned about different types of diagrams, and consider the inherent difficulties students might have with this type of visual.

1. _____

2. _____

3. _____

4. _____

5. _____

How might you teach this lesson? What types of diagrams and three-dimensional graphic organizers (and perhaps other visual literacy tools) would you have your students use to develop their knowledge—and demonstrate their understanding—of force and motion? Now is a good time to review Chapters 3, 4, and 5 for descriptions of the many visual tools available to you.

Figure 8.9 Graph of Animal Speeds (Zebra, Cheetah, Lion)

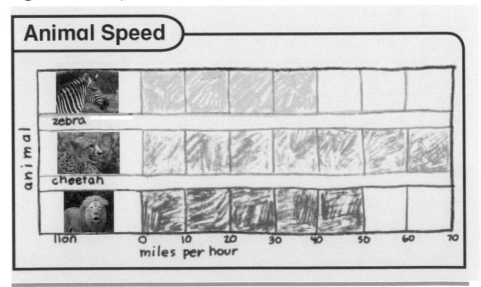

Source: Hackett, J. K., R. H. Moyer, and J. Vasquez. 2008. *Science A Closer Look.* Grade 2, Visual Literacy. Columbus, OH: Macmillan/ McGraw-Hill, p. 32. Copyright © 2008 Macmillan/McGraw-Hill. Reprinted with permission.

CHAPTER 9
Visual Literacy: Next Steps

In many of our professional development sessions, we show a cartoon that you may have seen. The cartoon shows two little boys talking and a very cute little dog sitting off to the side. One of the boys says, "I taught my dog how to whistle." The other boy responds, "I don't hear him whistling." The first boy answers, "I said I taught him. I didn't say he learned it."

Even if you have not seen the cartoon, you can visualize it, and certainly you can relate it to your classroom experiences. How often do we teach something only to find out later that students just didn't get it? The bigger question to ask is, Did the dog need to learn how to whistle? Of course not, as long as the dog responded to the boy's whistling and he knew what that meant.

This same metaphor can be applied to some of the skills we teach our students, many of which they, as 21st-century workers, will not need. Take cursive writing, for example. Kindergarten and first-grade teachers spend many classroom hours trying to get their students to become the best printers they can be. Then in second or third grade, we compound the time spent teaching handwriting by requiring students to learn cursive. It's nice to have great penmanship, but is it necessary? How often do you communicate via handwritten messages? Perhaps you use cursive for signing your name or sending thank-you notes. Today, tablet computers can decipher even the worst handwriting, converting it into text that can be manipulated into any font type, style, or size—or even into another language! Literacy itself will thrive, but it will be a different kind of literacy from what we experienced growing up.

Howard Gardner, a cognitive psychologist at the Harvard Graduate School of Education well-known for his theory of multiple intelligences, recently posed this question:

> What will happen to reading and writing in our time? Could the doomsayers be right? Computers, they maintain, are destroying literacy. The signs—students' declining reading scores, the drop in leisure reading to just minutes a week, the fact that half the adult population reads no books in a year—are all pointing to the day when a literate American culture becomes a distant memory. By contrast, optimists foresee the Internet ushering in a new, vibrant participatory culture of words. Will they carry the day? ... Let me suggest a third possibility: Literacy—or a variety of literacies—will continue to thrive, but in forms and formats we can't yet envision. (2008, p. B01)

As we have seen in this book, *literacy* is taking on different meanings. Today, being literate includes not just the ability to read, write, and do basic mathematics. Literacy has come to include much more: the ability to access, analyze, evaluate, and communicate in a variety of forms. Embedded in this definition are both a process for learning and an expansion of the concept of "text" that includes visual images. It is this written and visual text that provides the platform to help all students learn. Today's digital students who have Google at their fingertips may be able to find information quickly, but will they be able to discern and analyze what is needed to *know* and to *understand* the subject?

Teaching the Digital Natives

According to Daniel Pink (2005), two skills will make our students successful in adulthood: *high concept*, or the ability to detect patterns, connect unrelated ideas, and create something new, and *high touch,* or the ability to empathize, read faces and gestures, and inspire joy in oneself and others. Explicit teaching of visual literacy skills and methods of learning will help students use and present the information they discover in understandable, coherent, and concrete (graphical) ways. Research in both educational theory and cognitive psychology tells us that visual learning is among the very best methods for teaching students of all ages how to think and how to learn.

This "net" generation and the digital natives it has produced have grown up using digital media. Their brains are conditioned to use computers to play games, send e-mail, exchange instant messages, or videoconference. Instead of meeting face-to-face, they text one another on their cell phones or convey information through their postings on social bulletin boards and blogs. According to a recent study of 2,000 students between the ages of 8 and 18, the average student spends six hours a day connected to some digital communication device, often several simultaneously (Tapscott 2009). Even young students do homework while listening to iPods, sending instant messages, or watching movies on their computers. By the time they reach adolescence, they are experts at skimming and scanning. "The average person spends two seconds on a Web site when searching for information" (Small and Vorgan 2008, p. 28). Two seconds! Unfortunately, however, unless students are taught how to process, synthesize, and document information, it will only be retained for a few seconds and then lost and forgotten. Not retained. Not learned.

We hope that by reading this book you have acquired some ideas and techniques that can help you promote long-term learning in your students. Remember, visual learning helps students

- make abstract ideas visible and concrete;
- connect prior knowledge and new concepts;
- provide structure for thinking, writing, discussing, analyzing, planning, and reporting; and
- focus thoughts and ideas, leading to understanding and interpretation.

Visual literacy instruction should be an essential component of today's science teaching.

CHAPTER 9

Images and English Language Learners

After the last general U.S. Census in 2000, it was estimated that nine million children between the ages of five and seven speak a language other than English at home, and many of these children do not speak English well. If they do not become fluent speakers of English in preschool and kindergarten, they fall further and further behind and eventually drop out of high school. Teachers who provide knowledge only in written formats are setting up English language learners for failure. Because those students cannot rely solely on linguistic ability to learn and retain knowledge in a new language, nonlinguistic methods of learning are particularly important for them to succeed.

Using modes other than the English language to communicate has long been a mainstay in the tool kit of ELL teachers. To make English instruction as understandable as possible for the English language learner, teachers in mainstream classes should also use diverse media, including graphs, diagrams, photos, and maps, as well as hands-on experiences. To help ELL students learn the science vocabulary they need to know,

> students should be provided with multiple sources of information to learn words. Key vocabulary should be taught and reviewed more than once. Multiple sources of meaning should be provided. Real drawings, pictures, videos, gestures, and dramatization are examples of ways to provide sources of meaning other than the definition of the word. (Fathman and Crowther 2006, p. 44)

Hill and Flynn, in their book *Classroom Instruction That Works With English Language Learners* (2006, pp. 37–41), provide five recommendations for using nonlinguistic representations in the classroom.

1. **Use graphic organizers to represent knowledge.** Graphic organizers, which include diagrams, charts, webs, and timelines, can be designed to make complex content more understandable for the English language learner.

2. **Use symbolic representations, such as pictures, pictographs, maps, and diagrams to help students understand text.** For

English language learners to understand what they are reading, they must make the connections between text and concept that will help them comprehend the material. Pictographs can help students visualize information, recognize patterns, remember new content and vocabulary, and provide a link to what they already know.

3. **Help students generate mental pictures.** When they listen to a story or read a selection, it is important to help them create a "movie in their mind" that can provide them with a vehicle for understanding and a means for storing knowledge. This can provide the bridge between the words and the object they are studying.

4. **Make physical models.** Physical models, including three-dimensional forms, are concrete representations of what is being learned. The very act of constructing a concrete representation establishes an "image" of the knowledge, so the English language learner does not have to depend solely on words for building understanding.

5. **Engage students in kinesthetic activities in which they represent knowledge using physical movement.** Students can engage in active language learning by demonstrating their comprehension through body movements and dramatic play.

This list illustrates why it is important to allow your English language learners to demonstrate their understanding through nonlinguistic representations. It also illustrates that having visual literacy skills is a necessity not just for English language learners but for all the students in your classroom.

Summary Thoughts

Think about the students to whom you teach science. If you are an elementary teacher, you probably teach students who love to learn about the world around them. Ideally, your lessons have a hands-on and minds-on inquiry approach—you provide your students with many questions to think about and you encourage them to come up with their own questions. Middle school teachers, on the other hand, may be faced with students who have lost their zest for learning, perhaps because they had science classes in elementary school that were less than wonderful. They may come to you thinking that science is boring and that it is all about reading. As a teacher of science, you want your students to learn important scientific concepts as well as to use a thoughtful, methodical approach to their study of science. Visual literacy tools can be thought of as the synthesizers of ideas and as a method for engaging your students.

A strong case for the power of visual thinking is made in the unique book *Thinking in Pictures—And Other Reports From My Life With Autism,* by Temple Grandin (1996). Grandin has a PhD in animal science and has created numerous unique and highly successful inventions for use in the cattle industry. Grandin is a high-functioning autistic. She has, as she describes in her book, a remarkable capacity to form a virtual visual library in her mind: "Words are like a second language to me. I translate both spoken and written words into full-color movies, complete with sound, which run like a VCR tape in my head. When someone speaks to me, his words instantly translate into pictures" (p. 154).

Grandin may be an extraordinary example, but her experiences give us insight into basic human capacities. When Howard Gardner (1983, 1999) developed his theory of multiple intelligences, he looked at the far reaches of human capacities and extrapolated from these cases to reveal the capacities within all of us. Grandin's rich descriptions of her thinking processes are a magnification of what most of our students are able to do, given practice and the right tools. After kindergarten, most students are given lined paper on which to record their thinking. It's important that we also give them plenty of blank paper on which to draw pictures and construct other visual representations as a way to unlock their thinking processes.

REFERENCES

Anderson, L. W., and D. R. Krathwohl, eds. 2001. *A taxonomy for learning, teaching, and assessing: A revision of Bloom's taxonomy of educational objectives.* Boston: Allyn and Bacon/Pearson Education Group.

Ansberry, K., and E. Morgan. 2010. *Picture perfect science lessons, Expanded 2nd Edition: Using children's books to guide inquiry, 3–6.* Arlington, VA: NSTA Press.

Bloom, B. S., and D. R. Krathwohl. 1956. *Taxonomy of educational objectives: The classification of educational goals. Handbook I: Cognitive domain.* New York: Longmans, Green.

Bransford. J. D., A. L. Brown, and R. R. Cocking, eds. 2000. *How people learn: Brain, mind, experience and school.* Washington DC: National Academies Press.

Bybee, R. W., J. A. Taylor, A. Gardner, P. Van Scotter, J. Carlson Powell, A. Westbrook, and N. Landes. 2006. *The BSCS 5E instructional model: Origins, effectiveness, and applications.* Colorado Springs, CO: BSCS.

Caine, R. N., and G. Caine. 1994. *Making connections: Teaching and the human brain.* New York: Dale Seymour.

Chanlin, L. 1997. The effects of verbal elaboration and visual elaboration on student learning. *International Journal of Instructional Media* 24 (4): 333–339.

Debes, J. L. 1969. The loom of visual literacy. *Audiovisual Instruction* 14 (8): 25–27.

Douglas, R., M. Klentschy, and K. Worth. 2006. *Linking Science and Literacy in the K–8 Classroom.* Arlington, VA: NSTA Press.

Fadiman, C., ed. 1985. *The Little, Brown book of anecdotes.* Boston: Little, Brown.

Fathman, A., and D. Crowther, eds. 2006. *Science for English language learners: K–12 strategies.* Arlington, VA: NSTA Press.

Gardner, H. 1983. *Frames of mind: The theory of multiple intelligences.* New York: Basic Books.

Gardner, H. 1999. *Intelligence reframed: Multiple intelligences for the 21st century.* New York: Basic Books.

Gardner, H. *The Washington Post.* 2008. The End of Literacy? Don't Stop Reading. Feb. 17. Also available online at *www.washingtonpost.com/wp-dyn/content/article/2008/02/15/AR2008021502898.html*

Gazzaniga, M. 1998. *The mind's past.* Berkeley, CA: University of California Press.

REFERENCES

Gerlic, I., and N. Jausovec. 1999. Multimedia: Differences in cognitive processes observed with EEG. *Educational Technology Research and Development* 47 (3): 5–14.

Grandin, T. 1996. *Thinking in pictures—and other reports from my life with autism.* New York: Knopf Doubleday.

Hackett, J. K., R. H. Moyer, and J. Vasquez. 2008. *Science A Closer Look.* Columbus, OH: Macmillan/McGraw-Hill.

Harvey, S., and A. Goudvis. 2000. *Strategies that work.* 2nd ed. Portland, ME: Stenhouse Publishers.

Hill, J. D., and K. M. Flynn. 2006. *Classroom instruction that works with English language learners.* Alexandria, VA: ASCD.

Hyerle, D. 2004. *Student successes with thinking maps: School-based research, results, and models for achievement using visual tools.* Thousand Oaks, CA: Corwin Press.

Hyerle, D. 2009. *Visual tools for transforming information into knowledge.* Thousand Oaks, CA: Corwin Press.

Keeley, P., and R. Harrington. 2010. *Uncovering student ideas in physical science, vol. 1: 45 new force and motion assessment probes.* Arlington, VA: NSTA Press.

Klentschy, M. P. 2008. *Using science notebooks in elementary classrooms.* Arlington, VA: NSTA Press.

Klentschy, M. P. 2010. *Using science notebooks in middle school.* Arlington, VA: NSTA Press.

Koellner-Clark, K. 2003. Whodunit? Exploring proportional reasoning through the footprint problem. *School Science and Mathematics Education* 103 (2): 92–98.

Larson, B. 2009. Astronomies of scale. *Science and Children* 47 (2): 54–56.

Lehrer, R., and L. Schauble. 2006. Cultivating model-based reasoning in science education. In *Cambridge handbook of the learning sciences,* ed. K. Sawyer, 371–388. Cambridge, MA: Cambridge University Press.

Marzano, R. J., D. J. Pickering, and J. E. Pollock. 2001. *Classroom instruction that works: Research-based strategies for increasing student achievement.* Alexandria, VA: ASCD.

McKenzie, J. 1998. Grazing the Net: Raising a generation of free-range students. *Phi Delta Kappan* 80 (1): 26–31. Also available at *www.fno.org/text/grazing/html*

Michaels, S., A. W. Shouse, and H. A. Schweingruber. 2008. *Ready, set, science! Putting research to work in the K–8 science classroom.* Washington, DC: National Academies Press.

Moline, S. 1995. *I see what you mean: Children at work with visual information.* Portland, ME: Stenhouse Publishers.

Moore, C. F., J. A. Dixon, and B. A. Haines. 1991. Components of understanding in proportional reasoning: A fuzzy set representation of developmental progressions. *Child Development* 62: 441–459.

National Center on Education and the Economy (NCEE). 2008. *Tough choices or tough times: The report of the New Commission on the Skills of the American Workforce.* Washington, DC: NCEE.

National Research Council (NRC). 1996. *National science education standards.* Washington. DC: National Academies Press.

National Research Council (NRC). 2006. *Learning to think spatially: GIS [geographic information system] as a support system in the K–12 curriculum.* Washington, DC: National Academies Press.

Paivio, A. 1991. Dual coding theory: Retrospect and current status. *Canadian Journal of Psychology* 45 (3): 255–287.

Pink, D. H. 2005. *A whole new mind: Moving from the information age to the conceptual age.* New York: Penguin Group.

Pinto, R., and J. Ametller. 2002. Students' difficulties in reading images: Comparing results from four national research groups. *International Journal of Science Education* 24 (3): 333–341.

Roblyer, M. D. 1998. Visual literacy: Seeing a new rationale for teaching with technology. *Learning and Leading with Technology* 26 (2): 51–54.

Small G., and G. Vorgan. 2008. *iBrain: Surviving the technological alteration of the modern mind.* New York: HarperCollins.

Stokes, S. 2002. Visual literacy in teaching and learning: A literature perspective. *Electronic Journal for the Integration of Technology in Education* 1 (1).

Tapscott, D. 2009. *Growing up digital.* New York: McGraw-Hill.

Tate, M. 2010. *Worksheets don't grow dendrites: 20 instructional strategies that engage the brain.* 2nd ed. Thousand Oaks, CA: Corwin Press.

Van Gogh, V. *www.vangoghgallery.com/misc/quotes.html*

Wisconsin State Superintendent of Public Instruction. 2009. Math glossary of terms. Madison, WI: Wisconsin State Department of Public Instruction. *http://dpi.wi.gov/standards/mathglos.html*

Wolfe, P. 2004. Foreword. In *Student Success With Thinking Maps,* ed. D. Hyerle, S. Curtis, and L. Alper. Thousand Oaks, CA: Corwin Press.

Worth, K., J. Winokur, S. Cressman, M. Heller-Winokur, and M. Davis. 2009. *Science and literacy: A natural fit. A guide for professional development leaders.* Portsmouth, NH: Heinemann.

Zike, D. 2000. *Dinah Zike's foldables for grades 1–6: 3-D interactive organizers.* New York: Macmillan/McGraw Hill.

Zike, D. 2006. *Dinah Zike's teaching with foldables: Science and mathematics.* San Antonio, TX: Dinah-Might Adventures, LP.

Zike, D. 2008. *Notebook foldables (for spirals, binders, and composition books).* San Antonio, TX: Dinah-Might Adventures, LP.

OTHER RESOURCES

Burmark, L. 2002. *Visual literacy: Learn to see, see to learn.* Alexandra, VA: ASCD.

Cook, M. 2008. Students' comprehension of science concepts depicted in textbook illustrations. *Electronic Journal of Science Education* 12 (1): 1–14.

Dimopoulos, K., V. Koulaidis, and S. Sklaveniti. 2003. Towards an analysis of visual images in school science textbooks and press articles about science and technology. *Research in Science Education* 33: 189–216.

Fogarty, J., and J. Stoehr. 1995. *Integrating curricula with multiple intelligences: Teams, themes and threads.* Arlington Heights, IL: IRI Skylight Training and Publishing.

Forceville, C. 1999. *Educating the eye.* Thousand Oaks, CA: Sage Publications.

Gangwer, T. 2009. *Visual impact, visual teaching: Using images to strengthen learning.* Thousand Oaks, CA: Corwin Press.

Gordin, D. N., and R. Pea. 1995. Prospects for scientific visualization as an educational technology. *Journal of Learning Sciences* 4 (3): 249–279.

Hyerle, D. 1996. *Visual tools for constructing knowledge.* Alexandria, VA: ASCD.

Hyerle, D. 2000. *A field guide to using visual tools.* Alexandria, VA: ASCD.

Jensen. E. 1998. *Teaching with the brain in mind.* Alexandria, VA: ASCD.

Kress, G. 2003. *Literacy in the new media age.* New York: Routledge.

Marzano, R. J. 2007. *The art and science of teaching: A comprehensive framework for effective instruction.* Alexandria, VA: ASCD.

Mayer, R. E., W. Bove, A. Bryman, R. Mars, and L. Tapangco. 1996. Why less is more: Meaningful learning from visual and verbal summaries of science textbook lessons. *Journal of Educational Psychology* 88 (1): 64–73.

Messaris, P. 1994. *Visual literacy: Image, mind, and reality.* Boulder, CO: Westview Press.

National Research Council (NRC). 2005. *How students learn: Science in the classroom.* Washington, DC: National Academies Press.

Paulu, N. 1991. *Helping your child learn science.* Washington, DC: U.S. Department of Education, Office of Educational Research and Improvement. *www2.ed.gov/pubs/parents/Science/Concepts.html*

OTHER RESOURCES

Ramadas, J. 2009. Visual and spatial modes in science leaning. *International Journal of Science Education* (Special Issue: "Visual and Spatial Modes in Science Learning") 31 (3): 301–318. This journal is online at *http://journalsonline.tandf.co.uk.*

Restak, R. 2001. *The secret life of the brain.* Washington, DC: The Dana Press and the Joseph Henry Press (an imprint of the National Academies Press).

Tretter, T. R., M. G. Jones, T. Andre, A. Negishi, and J. Minogue. 2006. Conceptual boundaries and distances: Students' and experts' concepts of the scale of scientific phenomena. *Journal of Research in Science Teaching* 423 (3): 282–319.

Unsworth, L. 2001. *Teaching multiliteracies across the curriculum: Changing contexts of text and image in classroom practice.* Berkshire, UK: Open University Press.

Vasquez, J. 2008. *Tools and traits for highly effective science teaching, K–8.* Portsmouth, NH: Heinemann.

Wiggins, G., and J. McTighe. 1998. *Understanding by design.* Alexandria, VA: ASCD.

Wolfe, P. 2001. *Brain matters: Translating research into classroom practice.* Alexandria, VA: ASCD.

Wurman, R. S. 1989. *Information anxiety: What to do when information doesn't tell you what you need to know.* New York: Bantam Books.

Index

*Page numbers in **boldface** type refer to figures.*